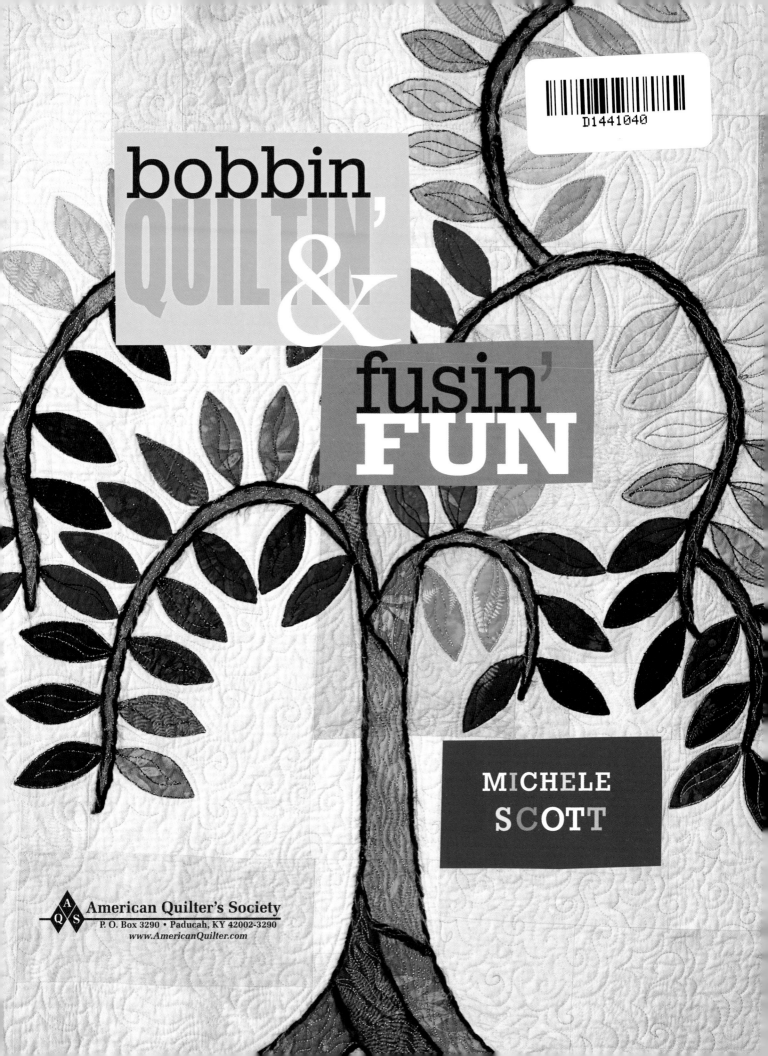

bobbin, QUILTIN' & fusin' FUN

MICHELE SCOTT

American Quilter's Society
P. O. Box 3290 • Paducah, KY 42002-3290
www.AmericanQuilter.com

Located in Paducah, Kentucky, the American Quilter's Society (AQS) is dedicated to promoting the accomplishments of today's quilters. Through its publications and events, AQS strives to honor today's quiltmakers and their work and to inspire future creativity and innovation in quiltmaking.

EXECUTIVE BOOK EDITOR: ANDI MILAM REYNOLDS
SENIOR EDITOR: LINDA BAXTER LASCO
COPY EDITOR: CHRYSTAL ABHALTER
GRAPHIC DESIGN: ELAINE WILSON
COVER DESIGN: MICHAEL BUCKINGHAM
QUILT PHOTOGRAPHY: CHARLES R. LYNCH
HOW-TO PHOTOGRAPHY: MICHELE SCOTT

Additional copies of this book may be ordered from the American Quilter's Society, PO Box 3290, Paducah, KY 42002-3290, or online at www.AmericanQuilter.com.

Text © 2011, Author, Michele Scott
Artwork © 2011, American Quilter's Society

LIBRARY OF CONGRESS CATALOGING-IN-PUBLICATION DATA

Scott, Michele, 1967-
  Bobbin quiltin' & fusin' fun / by Michele Scott.
    p. cm.
  ISBN 978-1-60460-006-3
  1. Machine quilting--Patterns. 2. Patchwork--Patterns. I. Title. II.
Title: Bobbin quiltin' and fusin' fun.
  TT835.S35925 2011
  746.46'041--dc23
                    2011033784

❀ Dedication ❀

For my husband, Tom. You have been a constant voice of loving support even when I failed to hear or listen well. You are my world.

❖ Acknowledgements ❖

There's a saying "it takes a village to raise a child"....or is it "there's a village missing its idiot?" In any case, the one thing I do know is that any success I've achieved in quilting or in life is due to the wonderful people who surround me. Their generosity and love overwhelm me on a daily basis. I am truly blessed.

A special and loving thank you to my mother, Elinore Locke. Her love of fiber arts was evident in our house. I was lucky to grow up in such a creative and inspiring environment...and it ultimately resulted in this book.

Thank you to my second best employee, Vicki Smith. You have picked me up every time I have fallen and have been my biggest cheerleader. In a lifetime, I will never be able to thank you for everything you've done for me.

A thank you to my contributors; Lacey Hill, Janet Saulsbury, Cyndi Souder, and Barbara Campbell. This book would not be as great without your input. I am blessed to have such talent assisting me with this daunting undertaking. And Lacey, I do owe you my first-born. An enormous thank you to Kay Ford-Sollimo, my astonishing proofreader. No matter how last minute I was, she was a superwoman!

Over 10 years ago, I decided I wanted to become a quilt professional. Linda Hahn and Merry May were generous with both their time and talent to help me get going in the right direction. I thank them for that.

To all the broads on the *McCall's Quilting* staff, especially (but not limited to!) Beth Hayes and Tricia Camp. During the past 11 years, you've been a pleasure to work for and have turned into dear friends. Thanks for putting up with my nonsense.

Thanks to the whole Northcott crew: Brian, Laurie, Hania, Patti, and Bernie. Working with all of you has been an experience of a lifetime. I am proud and honored to be on your team. A very special thank you to my art director and mentor, Deborah Edwards, a dear friend and teacher. You make everything I design so amazing.

Thank you to Rob McIlvaine for never making me feel too important.

To the whole AQS staff, especially Linda Lasco and Andi Reynolds. Your hard work catapulted my art to new heights. Thank you for believing in me and my dream.

To Tom and Peg McColligan. Thank you for welcoming me into your family with open arms and your unconditional love.

And last but never least, to my dad, Joseph Locke—your courage and determination inspire me to new heights.

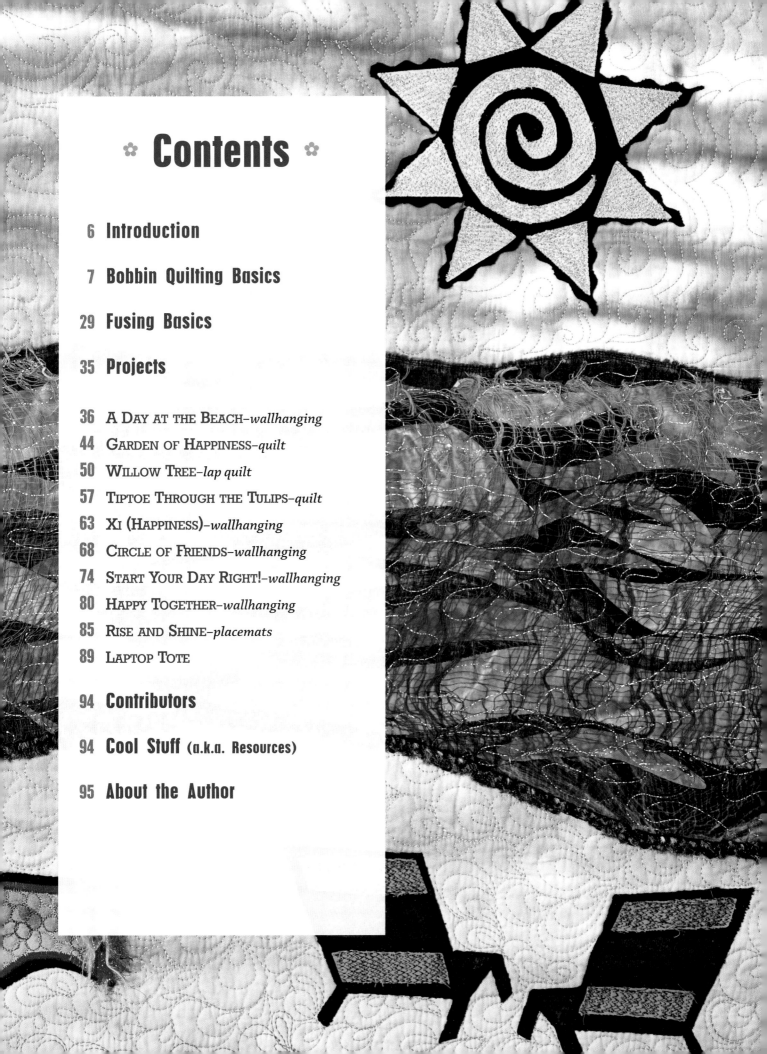

❀ Contents ❀

❀ Introduction ❀

There's one thing I love to do in quilting and another thing I despise. Those two emotions are the inspiration of this book. I love machine quilting and I hate piecing. It's as simple as that.

What draws me toward quilting most is the variety of threads that you can use to make your quilt jazzy and fun. There is an abundance of colorful and shimmery threads on the market today, and that in itself becomes a whole new obsession!

As I was trying out these new threads, I found that our delicate machines sometimes do not want to cooperate. The shredding and tearing is enough to make you want to toss them right out the window. But I would not be discouraged! Darn it, I paid good money for those threads and I was determined to make machine quilting work. That's what the first section of this book is all about. Why agonize over broken needles and tattered threads when you can throw them in the bobbin, flip over the quilt, and quilt it up-side-down?

As for piecing, I'm horrible at it. There, I admit it. I am definitely not that Type A personality because as I piece my blocks, they all seem to be different sizes. That's why fusing has been an amazing discovery for me. How easy is it to draw out your design, trace, iron, and cut it out? The room for error has just quadrupled! What I'm trying to say is that it is possible to create and finish works of art in a fraction of the time and

aggravation. I have found that the possibilities are endless.

The third section has 11 projects including bed quilts, lap quilts, wallhangings, bags, placemats—we have it all! You can perfect your bobbin quilting and fusing with the beautiful projects from a number of designers.

There is one important thing I want you to know before you begin this incredibly freeing journey. The information in this book is what I've found to be most successful for the many classes I've taught and for myself. It's not written in stone. As the old saying goes, "There's more than one way to skin a cat."

"Tips and tricks" came from experimentation. If this doesn't work, try that. If that way doesn't work, try another. This book is a compilation of that exact process. If you find something that does work, pursue it. Of course, I can't cover every thread, fusible, or product, but I've tried the majority that can be found on the market. The good news is that you can use these techniques with whatever you find. Before you know it, you won't just be a Fabriholic, you'll be a Threadaholic like me!

Remember: There are no Quilt Police. Let go of the need for perfection and you will find that the perfection will come. Free your mind and yourself and you will produce beauty.

Bobbin Quilting Basics

❀ ❀ ❀ ❀ ❀ ❀ ❀

Bobbin quilting involves putting decorative thread (or any thread, for that matter) in the bobbin and free-motion quilting your project with the backing facing up and the top upside down. Get it? If not, you soon will!

Why you would want to bobbin quilt?

- ◉ You can quilt with any thread that's on the market now.

- ◉ Broken needles and shredded threads will be a thing of the past.

Think about it. Thread on the top has to wind around a bunch of apparatus, through tension discs, and through a tiny little hole. It then jumps up and down at amazing speeds. Do we really think that fragile little thread is going to put up with that? When you put that thread in the bobbin, all it has to do is go through one tension disc. The threads prefer that SO much more!

- ◉ I feel that threads lie on the top of the fabric a little nicer when they come up from the bobbin. They seem to pucker less when you bobbin quilt.

- ◉ Not sure what pattern to quilt on your top? Choose a fabric with a great allover design and use it as the backing. Bobbin quilt following that design. You'll have a great design on the top of your quilt! (See Figs. 1–1a and 1b, pages 8–9).

Bobbin Quilting Basics ✿ ✿ ✿ ✿ ✿ ✿ ✿

Starting Machine Quilting—A Pep Talk

Before we jump into bobbin quilting, let's start with the basics of free-motion machine quilting. What do beginning quilters want the most? An item that will make them machine quilt perfectly. It ain't gonna happen! There are many great notions on the market that can aid you; some products can make the quilting easier, but there is no one item that will make you better. There's only one thing that will make you better. I know you don't want to hear it because you've heard it before...**Practice, Practice, Practice.**

I cannot emphasize enough how important it is to try new techniques repeatedly. Do not be discouraged by your early attempts. When you first begin, you may have many problems and never think it will get any easier, but it does. Just like anything that is worth it, you must keep at it.

According to a new study of success written by Malcolm Gladwell, in order to be successful at something, you don't need natural talent. What appears to be far more important is dedication and perseverance; dedication to keep on practicing and improving. Alex Anderson says that it takes about 100 hours.

You CAN do it if you put in the time. It doesn't have to be just boring practice. Make small quilts with easy piecing or, better yet, fusing. When you give them away as gifts, people will be thrilled! Volunteer to finish some of your guild's charity quilts. Recipients won't see the uneven stitches or knots. All they will see is a beautiful handmade quilt.

✿ **tip:**

Busy Backs! Always back your project with a fabric that has an intricate design. This way it's that much more difficult to see less than perfect stitches!

LEFT AND OPPOSITE: Figs. 1–1a and 1b. Choose a fabric with a great allover design and quilt it from the back.

Take as many classes as you can. Books are excellent resources, but nothing can compare to being with an instructor when something is not going exactly as planned. Machine quilting is a different kind of technique class because every machine is different. Not all problems are the same and it helps to have someone with you who is familiar with the speed bumps. Another good option is to check with friends who machine quilt. You can benefit from their mistakes and learn something new as well.

Clean and oil your machine frequently and start with a new needle on every new project. A good rule of thumb is to change your needle about every 8 hours of machine quilting.

You may want to make up some practice pieces that are nothing more than your batting sandwiched between two pieces of muslin. These practice pieces can be used to practice starting and stopping, adjusting tension and stitch length, and eventually to practice your freeform designs. Keep a record of the threads, tensions, and anything that you have found successful. This way, if you have been away from your machine for a while, you can recreate your best work with ease. You may want to start a binder where you can save some of your practice pieces, especially where you like the result. Use a permanent marker to write notes on each piece.

Make sure you BREATHE! It is easy to be caught up in what you are doing and find yourself holding your breath. Get a rhythm. Listen to your favorite music and let the music guide you through your work. You may find that singing along helps you relax. You may prefer to sew while you listen to TV, a movie, or books on tape. Sometimes a quiet house is the best inspiration.

Do not go for hours at a time; interrupt yourself on a regular basis! Get up, stretch, and move around. It is easy to get into your project and not realize that you have been hunched over your machine for hours. Take a deep breath, move your shoulders down from around your ears, straighten your upper back, and move your neck around. This will improve your stitches and prevent you from being stiff and sore the next day.

For larger projects, you will have to find a way to work with the extra bulk, or you may find that you just do not enjoy working on very large projects, or that you can only sew for shorter periods of time on them.

All right....enough of the pep talk. Let's get into the meat and potatoes of this.

Machine Quilting Tools

These tools will make your quilting easier, whether you are quilting from the top or the bobbin.

WALKING FOOT (ALSO CALLED AN EVEN FEED OR DUAL FEED FOOT)

This is the foot you put on your machine when you want to do straight-line quilting. It aids in feeding your quilt evenly through the machine. I don't use it very often because when you need to turn a corner, you have to turn the entire quilt. If I need to "draw" a straight line, I will do it via free motion. It's difficult at first, but the more you do it, the easier it is. I use the walking foot for couching yarns onto my quilt and for sewing on the binding.

DARNING FOOT (ALSO CALLED FREE-MOTION FOOT)

This is my main foot. When you drop (or cover) the feed dogs, you can machine quilt in any direction without turning the quilt. It applies no pressure to the quilt so you can move it easily. Different manufactures use different feet, so make sure to consult your machine dealer to find the right one for your machine.

SECOND BOBBIN CASE

Whether you have a front-loading or drop-in bobbin, it is a good idea to get an extra bobbin case. If you're using thicker threads, it's essential to loosen the bobbin case's tension. I've had students who could not get their tension back to its original setting. Mark your second case with fingernail polish so as not to get them mixed up. (There's more on tension starting on page 15.)

> ✿ tip:
>
> If a thread can go through the top (size 12 or higher), it can go through the bobbin with **no** bobbin case adjustments. Just wind, load, and sew!

NEEDLES

I believe that this is one of the most essential tools for successful machine quilting. I have found that you only need one type of needle, no matter what thread you are using—the Topstitch needle. My students ask me all the time what makes it so different, so great? I tell them that it is either fairy dust or a larger groove in the needle that helps accommodate thread and protect it from the activity your machine is inflicting on it.

Other needles are effective: Embroidery, Quilting, Metafil, Metallic, Metallica. I have tried them all. Some are good for one thread, another for something else. But I have found the Topstitch works for all threads. The higher the number on the needle, the larger the hole (which is the opposite of thread sizes). For thinner threads, I use 90/14. For thicker threads, up to size 12, I use a 100/16 needle.

And please, I beg of you, please…change your needle frequently. Not changing the needle is another common mistake people make. Old needles can cause skipped stitches, shredding threads, and noisy machine work. As a rule of thumb, I change my needle after every project OR if I'm having any problems at all with my quilting.

BATTING

I prefer cotton batting. Cotton has a wonderful drape and a soft hand. Cotton "breathes," creating a cooling effect in the summer and natural warmth in the winter. I'm a fan of a Fairfield batting called Machine 60/40 Blend® Batting of 60% cotton and 40% special blend polyester. What makes it so special is that it is less likely to hold a "fold" in your quilt. This is especially good for quilts you're sending to shows.

A new favorite of mine is Nature-Fil™ Blend Quilt Batting, also from Fairfield. A unique blend of 50% rayon fiber from bamboo and 50% certified organic cotton creates a quilt batting with a luxuriously soft hand and smooth drape. The light scrim allows for dense machine quilting while retaining its shape and softness, making it ideal for art quilts and wallhangings.

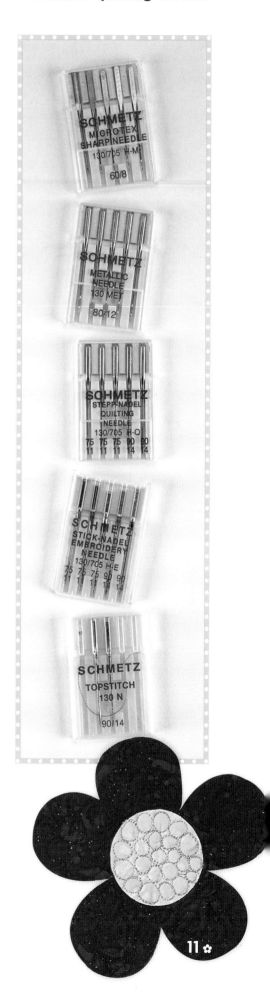

BASTING

I think my least favorite task in the whole quiltmaking process is basting (securing all three layers together prior to quilting), so I am a huge fan of spray basting my medium to small quilts. I especially love 505® Spray & Fix Temporary Fabric Adhesive from J. T. Trading. It is a repositionable fabric adhesive used to temporarily bond fabric. It is odorless, colorless, and does not gum up sewing machine needles. I not only use it for basting, but other things I cover in the book. For larger quilts, use stainless steel safety pins. Never thread baste because it's too difficult to pull out the threads!

Lay your batting (cut to size) on the floor. Spray the batting and place your quilt top, right side up, on top of the sprayed batting. Turn the batting and quilt top over and spray the other side of the batting. Place the backing on the batting, right side up. Press the quilt sandwich on both sides to relieve any extra fullness. Continue to press after quilting an area. This ensures a quilt free of wrinkles.

In many of the quilts, it's not necessary for the pieces to be fused prior to basting. When you use the lightweight fusible products, sometimes the pieces will not hold up to the entire quilting process. All of the manipulation sometimes detaches the pieces. Baste the quilt prior to fusing and fuse as you quilt.

You may notice in some of these projects that the batting and backing are significantly larger than the quilt top. In these cases, the borders will be fused on to the quilt top *and* the batting.

MARKING TOOLS

I don't mark. I find that trying to follow a line is too difficult. If I have a certain design in mind that I want to put in each area, marking is a necessity. To do this, I prefer Golden Threads Quilting Paper. Draw/trace your design on the paper, position on your quilt, and quilt through the paper. It tears away cleanly and easily without pulling out the stitches. You can also use a very lightweight tracing paper or that paper doctors use to cover their examination tables. There are many other great marking tools on the market, but it makes me very nervous to mark anything on my finished quilts.

TRACTION TOOLS

Your hands are soft and fabric is soft. That's a tough combination for moving a quilt sandwich. The bigger the quilt, the harder it is. I use gloves with little "nubbies" on them that grip the fabric and make it easier to move. There are many types on the market, but I use good ole' gardening gloves. They are much cheaper and just as good! I cut off the tips of the fingers to make working with the thread easier. Another great product is Lickity Grip®. Applied to your fingers, it is an agent that attracts moisture to give you a better grip on your fabric for better control of your quilting. It does almost the same thing as the gloves, but without wearing the gloves!

YOU GOTTA HAVE SUPPORT!

Some machines have support tables that come with the machine. It is imperative to have that larger area to aid in manipulating the quilt. If your machine doesn't have one, there are many companies that create acrylic portable tables with adjustable legs custom fit for your machine. They come in all shapes and sizes—just "Google" and you'll find them. My personal favorite is the cabinet into which the machine is placed so that it is flush with the top. Regardless of the machine or table, make sure that you have a table or area to support the weight of your quilt sandwich. Weight can be an annoying hindrance to successful stitching. I've even used an ironing board to support the overflow weight of a quilt that my table couldn't hold. Be sure that when you prepare your quilt, you roll the excess quilt neatly and tightly so it fits under the arm of your machine, giving you more room to work.

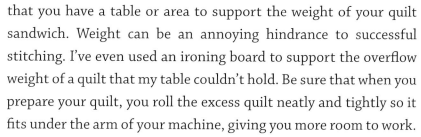

Let's Start!

Let's begin with the basics. We will start by working on basic machine quilting and getting the stitch just right. Start with two 16" x 16" muslin squares with cotton batting sandwiched between the two. Put a basic cotton thread in the top and bobbin of your machine. Be sure that the threads contrast with each other and with the muslin so you can see how the tension is working.

> ✿ **tip:**
> Be sure to thread the top of your machine with your presser foot UP. When the foot is down, all of the tension discs are engaged and you won't thread through them, resulting in bad tension.

> ✿ **tip:**
>
> Just learning machine quilting? For the love of Pete, start with a smaller quilt. It's hard enough learning how to get the rhythm and stitches just right, let alone trying to wrestle with a queen-size quilt to boot! There are some really great small projects here that you can start with. The less bulk you have in the beginning, the better. Work your way up to the larger stuff.

When you thread your machine with the top thread, the presser foot must be in the up position. When the presser foot is down, the tension discs inside the machine are engaged, and the thread will ride over and not between them. You definitely won't get good tension then!

Drop (or cover) your feed dogs and attach the darning foot.

Set your machine to stop in the needle-down position. When you stop, your needle will remain in the sandwich and keep it from shifting.

If you are a beginner, it is best to adjust your machine speed to half. Consult your manual to see if your machine has this feature.

Place your sandwich under the darning foot and lower the presser foot.

While holding the top thread, manually rotate the flywheel toward you in one complete rotation so that the needle is back in its highest position. The bobbin thread will be looped around the top thread. Raise the darning foot and draw up your bobbin thread to the top by pulling on the top thread. Place both threads toward the back of the foot. You have to bring up the bobbin thread because it can get caught up on the back while you quilt. This is especially important when you begin bobbin quilting. Take a few stitches in place to tack the threads, then clip the tails (see Figs. 1–2a and b).

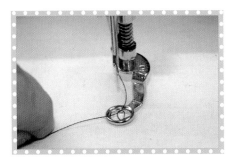

Fig. 1–2a

Lower the foot and begin stitching your sandwich. Remember, your movement determines the stitch length. If you run your machine fast and move the sandwich slowly, you will create tiny, tiny stitches and affect the thread tension dramatically. If you run your machine slowly and move the sandwich quickly, your stitches will be huge and not very smooth at all (see Fig. 1–3, page 15).

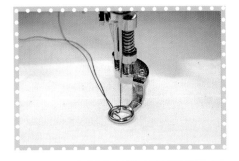

Fig. 1–2b

Find that right speed and concentrate on making your stitches as even as possible. It will be difficult at first, but persevere.

Practice your stitching all over the sandwich, moving it forward, backwards, and sideways. Do not turn or rotate the sandwich at all. With a larger quilt, you can't turn, so don't get in the habit of doing so. Start with curves. The majority of our designs are curved, so work on smooth, curved lines. Practice writing your name! (Fig. 1–4) Keep at it until you feel good about it!

Secure the threads in the same manner as you began, by tacking and clipping the ends. NOTE: When using thicker threads OR if you plan to enter the quilt in a contest, it is important to tie and tuck the beginning and ending threads (see page 20).

Fig. 1–4

PERFECTING THE TENSION!

Some people are afraid to adjust ANYTHING on their machine. Please trust me...when you adjust the top tension, it will not affect any of the machine's settings. The set top tension is 4 for most machines, and there is always a "dash" either on the dial or through a computer setting. It can be easily reset. (Fig. 1–5).

Now that you are all set with stitching, let's work on creating the perfect tension for whatever thread you use! Keep in mind...if you have a thread whose tension refuses to cooperate, you can put that thread in the bobbin and bobbin quilt (see the next section).

Fig. 1–5

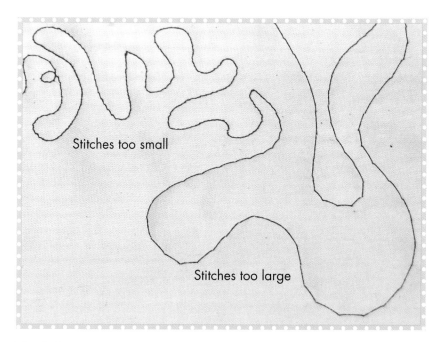

Stitches too small

Stitches too large

Fig. 1–3

❀ **tip:**

As you're learning how to machine quilt, begin with invisible (also called monofilament) thread. It's a great way to practice your skills without stressing over perfection. It comes in both nylon and polyester, but I prefer nylon by far. I've done so many quilts with invisible thread and have always been pleased with the results. I dare you to find mistakes! I prefer a good name brand nylon monofilament. If you go with a cheaper, no name brand, it will not work well at all. Take it from me!

Fig. 1–6

Fig. 1–7a and b

Fig. 1–8

1. Prepare another muslin quilt sandwich. With a permanent marker, create a grid of 3" x 3" squares. In each section, you will try a different thread (Fig. 1–6).

2. Take a look in your thread stash and pick something you never used but always wanted to—a rayon, metallic, invisible, or thicker thread (nothing larger than a size 12). Consult My Favorite Threads (pages 26–28) to see the vast array of threads available. Make sure the thread contrasts with the muslin top.

3. Wind a bobbin with a cotton thread that contrasts with the top thread. We **want** to see any tension mishaps. Any needle is fine at this point. I always go with the Topstitch, but it is good to practice with different things, so use whatever you have on hand. You may find something that works great for you and your machine.

4. Begin free-motion doodling. After you have a 3" square covered, take a look at both the top and back of the sandwich. You don't want to see the top thread on the bottom, or the bobbin thread on the top. Here's the rule for adjusting the tension:

- ♥ If you see dots of bobbin thread on the top, it means the top tension is too tight, so you need to **lower** the top tension number by one or two increments (Figs. 1–7a and b). I have found that in most free-motion situations, this is the case.

- ♥ If you see dots of top thread on the back, it means your top tension is too loose, so you need to **raise** the top tension number by one or two increments (Fig. 1–8).

> ✿ **tip:**
>
> Hit the reset button! I've found that you can correct tension problems, shredding threads, and breaking needles by rethreading your machine and bobbin. Just like in computers, this simple "reboot" is all you need!

5. Free-motion quilt another 3" section and take another look. Lower or raise the number another increment depending on the need. Continue in this fashion until you have a balanced stitch. Keep in mind that the threads are contrasting, so if there is just a tiny, tiny dot on either the top or bottom, it is fine. In a "real" project, your top and bobbin threads will be matching and something that small will go unnoticed.

6. With a permanent marker, write directly on the sandwich next to the stitch the type of thread you used and the type of needle and number. Continue with an array of threads. This sandwich can be a great reference tool for future projects (Fig. 1–9).

Even with this sample sandwich, it is important to test any or all threads before beginning any project! Even though I'm the queen of rushing through, I always make sure the thread is working properly before starting to quilt.

✿ **tip:**

Tension still an issue no matter what adjustment you make? It just may be your machine-quilting technique. I have found that jerky, small stitches make a major impact on the tension. Make sure your stitches are even and smooth before you attempt to work on your tension issues.

✿ **tip:**

Are you still having those annoying little thread dots on the back of your quilt from the top thread no matter how much you fiddle with the tension? I hate to admit it but sometimes that happens. I have an array of fabric markers in my bag o' tricks, so I can color those dots to match the back of the quilt. It's a little known, yet great tip.

Fig. 1–9

Bobbin Quilting!

We are ready to explore bobbin quilting now! Are you excited? I know I am! If you have a thread that keeps breaking in the top, or a thread whose tension just won't cooperate, or a gorgeous thick sparkly thread, you can put it in the bobbin!

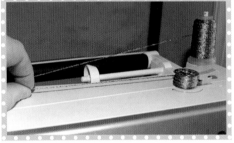

Fig. 1–10

Fig. 1–11

> ## ✿ tip:
>
> Invisible thread is especially good to use on bobbin quilting. With decorative thread in the bobbin and invisible thread on top, you're almost guaranteed to have that perfect tension look!
>
> I'm not a fan of using invisible thread in the bobbin, but try it! I know a lot of people who love using it in the bobbin.
>
>
>
> Quilting on the top
>
>
>
> Quilting on the back with invisible thread

ADJUSTING BOBBIN TENSION

Wind the thread onto the bobbin just as you would any other thread. You may want to go a little bit slower and keep a hand on the end of the thread as it winds (Fig. 1-10).

- **If you have a front-loading bobbin case:** Load the bobbin into your second (adjustable) bobbin case. Pull about 8" of thread out so the case is dangling (Fig. 1-11).

- Jerk the thread with your hand. You want the bobbin case to drop about 6" more, then stop. If the bobbin tension is too tight the thread will not unwind out of the case and the tension must be loosened. On the side of the bobbin case, you'll find a screw. Some bobbin cases have two screws, so always choose the larger screw.

Important! Please read! Before loosening the screw, be sure you are over an area that is contained and light. It is possible for the screw to pop out and roll to the land of the lost! I recommend that every time you adjust the screw, do it inside of a plastic baggie (Fig. 1-12). Some choose to do this over a towel or a bowl.

To loosen the bobbin tension, use the tiny little screwdriver that comes with your machine, and turn the screw to the left (remember: righty tighty, lefty loosey) a quarter turn. Reload the bobbin and let the bobbin case hang again. Jerk the thread as before. If it doesn't stop but keeps unwinding, you've loosened the tension too much. Tighten the screw just a bit. If it doesn't drop 6", keep adjusting by quarter turns until the bobbin drops in this manner.

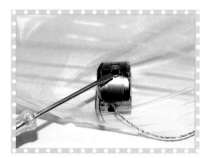

Fig. 1–12

If you have a top-loading bobbin case:

◉ Load the thread in the bobbin and pull on the thread. You will notice a lot of resistance in the thread. Remember how this feels. Find the screw on the side of your case. You are adjusting the screw that has a flat head, not Phillips head. In the same manner as above, turn the screw to the left a quarter turn from where you started (Fig. 1-13).

Fig. 1–13

◉ You will not be able to test the tension in the same manner as for a front-loading bobbin. Load the bobbin and pull the thread out. You will notice the difference from the first time you tested it. You want it to pull freely with some slack. You may have to go back and loosen it another quarter turn.

Fig. 1–14

STARTING TO QUILT

Now that your bobbin tension is just right, load the bobbin into its case and into the machine. Thread the top of the machine with the thread that will now be on the back of your quilt. Choose a thread that matches the bobbin thread (Fig. 1-14). If you're using a very thick thread, load your bobbin with invisible thread.

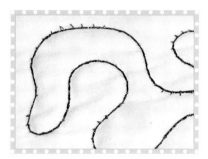

Fig. 1–15

Test stitch with the thread combination by machine quilting 3 square inches and take a look. If there are just dots on the top or bottom, you can lower or raise the top tension by one or two increments to get a balanced stitch (Fig. 1-15). If it is drastically uneven, you need to take out the bobbin and adjust the screw again. Don't get frustrated. Take your time and you will achieve magnificent results!

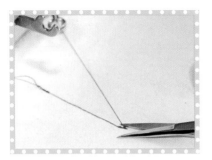

Fig. 1–16

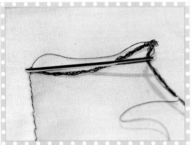

Fig. 1–17

Fig. 1–18

STARTING AND ENDING YOUR MACHINE QUILTING

There are two ways to start and end your machine quilting. The project you're working on or how much of a perfectionist you are will dictate the best method for you. The first is quick, easy and best used for quilts that are not going to be entered into a show and don't have thick threads. The second you should consider for show pieces.

Tacking: I usually will tack when using invisible thread because you can't see the tacking at all! The finish is not quite as polished as the tie and tuck method, but it's perfect if you're making a quilt for your Aunt Bessie!

After bringing the bobbin thread up from the bottom of the quilt, run a couple of stitches back and forth to tack the stitching. At the end of your quilting, run another couple of stitches to tack the end stitching. Cut threads close to the tacked stitch, both on bottom and top (Fig. 1-16).

Tie and Tuck: Very thick threads have to be tied and tucked. This method is also preferred for pieces entered in judged shows, regardless of the thread weight.

1. Start and end your stitching without any tacking at all. Be sure to leave a tail of thread at least 4" long at both ends.

2. Take the two beginning threads and tie them in a double knot. With either a tapestry or self-threading needle, bury the ends into your quilt top (Figs. 1-17 and 1–18).

3. At your end stitching, you need to either pull the bottom thread to the top or vice versa. As a general rule, the thinner thread pulls through more easily. Test both ways to see which is easier. In the same manner, knot the two threads and bury them into your quilt sandwich.

How the Heck Do I Know Where to Go?

When quilting from the back you need to know where to quilt. No worries! There are great techniques for this.

WHY BOTHER WITH ANYTHING? Do an allover pattern and it doesn't matter where you quilt! As mentioned previously, find a great design on a fabric and use it as backing for your quilt. Bobbin quilt following that design. How easy is that?

PIN IT! Surround the area on the top you want to quilt with very long, thin pins. When you turn the quilt over, you will see the backs of the pins around the desired quilting area. I like flower head pins. It can be a bit tricky because there have been times I hit the heads of the pins. It doesn't happen often, but it does happen! Oh well, not everything is foolproof! What I like about this method the most is that it is very quick and easy (Figs. 1-19a and 19b).

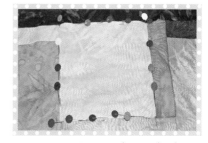

Fig. 1–19a. Area to be quilted, pinned around.

Fig. 1–19b. Back of quilt with pins showing

EVERYTHING BUT — I call it this because, quite simply, you machine quilt every area except the one where you want to do bobbin quilting. When you turn the quilt over, you can see the areas that need bobbin quilting. In this quilt I quilted all of the stars first. When the quilt was turned, I bobbin quilted around those star areas. This method, while effective, can be a bit tricky. I was sure to iron the fullness out to the edges after quilting 2–3 stars (Figs. 1-20a and 20b).

Figs. 1–20a and 20b. The star is quilted from the top so that when you turn the quilt to the back to bobbin quilt, you quilt all but the already quilted area.

a

b

With this method, you are quilting sections all over the quilt, not strictly from the center out. It is important to press the quilt after quilting several areas to ensure that all the extra fullness is pressed out.

INVISIBLE THREAD — Free-motion quilt around an area you want to bobbin quilt with invisible thread. The quilt is more secure and you can easily see the area from the back of the quilt.

WATER-SOLUBLE THREAD — Most major thread companies now carry thread that washes away in water. Similar to the concept of using invisible thread, you use it to stitch around the area to be quilted and you can see it from the back. You only need to use this thread on the top, because once the top washes away, the bobbin thread falls right off. This is preferred if you don't want quilting shown around the desired area.

MY PERSONAL FAVORITE: COUCHING! The couching technique involves sewing down a yarn, cord, or rickrack using invisible thread and a zigzag stitch. It serves a dual purpose. It not only livens up your quilt in the coolest way, but also shows you where to quilt on the back! I try to incorporate some type of couching in all my quilts. It's quick, easy, and adds one more interesting element to your piece. People are so impressed, which makes me laugh because that is usually the easiest part of the quilting process.

Couching

My students love couching. It's quick, easy and takes minutes to master! Since you are using a zigzag stitch, you need to raise your feed dogs to their original position and put on your walking foot. You need to have the walking foot on to feed all the layers smoothly and avoid puckering on the bottom. I know there are special couching "feet" for machines, but they're not necessary.

Set your machine to the zigzag stitch. Lengthen the stitch a couple of increments from the preset stitch. Load the machine with invisible thread on the top and cotton in the bobbin and stitch over the yarn or thread. You want the needle to clear each side, but not touch it (Fig. 1–21).

When turning a corner or at a point, position the needle down on the inside of the yarn/cord and turn the piece to continue. You should have a nice sharp angle (Fig. 1–22).

Sometimes a yarn that has a lot of smaller yarns or decorations can get matted down during the couching process. Use your hand and rub quickly over the yarn and the decorative pieces will pop up.

If you are couching a very wide yarn, ribbon, or rickrack, stitch down the middle with the straight stitch. Do not use a zigzag stitch because it may "tunnel" the embellishment (Fig.1–23).

Start and stop in the same way as in machine quilting—either tack the threads or tie and tuck. Whichever tickles your fancy!

I do a lot of couching of over fused pieces. At times, this can be tricky. The best rule of thumb is to always place the yarn/cord just inside the raw edge. If you place it directly on the raw edge, there is a danger of the cord popping off the edge. It's easier to trim away that raw edge if you go too far into the piece (Fig. 1–24).

For fun, couch the lines of an asymmetrical grid and fill each section with a different stitch using different decorative threads (Fig. 1–25, page 24).

Fig. 1–21

Fig. 1–22

Fig. 1–23

Fig. 1–24

Fig. 1–25

Geometric Swirls

Great border designs

My Favorite Doodles

Here are some of my favorite free-motion designs that don't need marking. I keep a notepad with me and doodle my ideas in my free time. When you practice on paper, it seems that your brain wraps around the movements and makes it that much easier to do it on your quilt. Practicing on paper can really sharpen your skills before doing the real thing. As much as you may love these doodles, don't try to copy them exactly. Just use the designs as a guide and go for it!

Geometric stipple

Stipple

Clouds

Swirls and points

Feathers

Large stipple (meadering)

Meandering stars

Circles

Swirls and points

Meandering swirls

Rectangular fingers

Overlapping lines

Curlicue meander

Waves

Flowering vines

Circles in circles

Back and forth

> ✿ **tip:**
>
> If you are using a thicker thread (anything size 12 or a lower number), you must slow down the machine speed a bit and make longer stitches. These threads are very thick and will be too jumbled on the top if you use your usual stitch. A longer stitch will make the thread look much better.

My Favorite Threads

You'll see in the chart that I generally prefer YLI brand threads, but all brand name threads have a product similar to the ones listed. You can find them on the Internet. The smaller the number of the thread, the thicker the thread. The lowest (thickest) thread that can go through the top of the machine is a size 12. Anything lower needs to go in the bobbin.

Not all threads have a number listed on them, so if you're not sure of the thread size, try it! You'll find out soon enough if it doesn't work through the top. Try these threads on our machine quilting exercises. Keep notes on the muslin practice pieces to keep as reference. Unless otherwise noted, I use a cotton thread in the bobbin that matches the color of the top thread. And as always, test the thread before using on your project!

HAPPY TOGETHER, detail. Full quilt on page 80.

My Favorite Threads		
Thread	**Description/Weight**	**Things to Know**
YLI Wonder Invisible thread	• .004 monofilament nylon	• Use Topstitch 90/14 needle. • Use in top (especially great when bobbin quilting) or bobbin. • Use with zigzag stitch to couch yarns/thick threads. • Top tension generally needs to be lowered. • Can be used for all quilts, with the exception of baby quilts.
YLI Machine Quilting Thread	• Size 40, 3-ply, 100% long staple cotton • 25 solid colors • 25 variegated colors	• Use Topstitch 90/14 needle. • Can be used in top or bobbin. • Long staple cotton; very easy to use in the machine. • Recommended for beginning machine quilters who aren't ready to use decorative threads, yet want a multicolored look. • Minor top tension adjustments may be needed. • Good for all quilts.
Superior Threads King Tut Thread	• Size 40, 3-ply, 100% extra long staple Egyptian cotton • Hundreds of variegated colors with an inch color change interval.	• Use Topstitch 90/14 needle. • Can be used in top or bobbin. • Like YLI Machine Quilting thread, it is very easy to use in the machine. • Short change color intervals mean that the colors will flow beautifully through your quilt. • Longarm quilters especially love this thread because of its low lint. • Minor top tension adjustments may be needed. • Good for all quilts.
Sulky Rayon	• Comes in sizes 40 and 30 • Hundreds of colors available including variegated and "twists." "Twists" are 2 rayon colors twisted together.	• Use Topstitch 90/14 needle. • Can be used in top or bobbin. • Minor top tension adjustments may be needed. • Rayon is very strong: can be used for all quilts. • A great way to add sheen to a quilt.
YLI Fine Metallic	• Size 40 • 23 colors including some twisted colors	• Use Topstitch 90/14 needle. • Can be used in top or bobbin. • Minor top tension adjustments may be needed. • In my opinion, the best metallic on the market because of minimal breakage. • Good for wall or lap quilts. • Produces a very subtle, pretty shine.
YLI Jeans Stitch	• Size 30 (although it has a thicker appearance), 100% spun polyester • 25 solid colors • 4 variegated colors	• Use Topstitch 100/16 needle. • Can be used in top or bobbin. • Produces a rich, colorful line. • Creates a soft, matte finish that is good for all quilts. • Use a longer stitch when machine quilting because of the thickness of thread.

Bobbin Quilting Basics ✿✿✿✿✿✿✿

Thread	Description/Weight	Things to Know
Flat Polyester Film	• Often called a metallic thread, it is actually a thin, flat ribbon-like polyester film that is metalized with aluminum to make it brilliantly reflective. • Variety of brands and colors	• Use Topstitch 90/14 needle. • Can be used in top, but frequently breaks in many machines. I just put it in the bobbin to avoid frustration. • Since it is a thin ribbon, you must use it on the vertical spool holder. When horizontal, it twists. • If you don't have a vertical spool holder for your machine, use the SideWinder™, a portable bobbin winder (see Resources, page 94). • Brands include Sulky Sliver, YLI Kaleidoscope, and Superior Threads Glitter. • Good for wall or lap quilts. • Produces a gorgeous sparkle.
Aurifil Lana Wool Thread	• Size 12, 50% wool and 50% acrylic (for strength) • 180 colors	• Use Topstitch 100/16 needle. Use a longer stitch when machine quilting because of the thickness of thread. • Can be used in top or bobbin but best results yield from the bobbin. • It is a strong, high quality wool; wonderfully soft and fluffy. • Use a longer stitch when machine quilting because of the thickness of thread. • Creates a soft, matte finish that is good for all quilts.
Artfabrik Hand-Dyed Cotton	• Assortment of variegated colors and sizes: 12 (top or bobbin) 8 (bobbin) 5 (couched) 3 (couched)	• Use Topstitch 100/16 needle with size 12. • Size 8 must be put in a bobbin case that's been loosened. • By far, my absolute favorite thread of all time. Hand-dyed by Laura Wasilowski, it comes in a rainbow of colors. Purchase on skeins; wind sizes 12 and 8 by hand onto spool. • Use a longer stitch when machine quilting because of the thickness of thread. • Strong cotton thread that can be used in all quilts.
YLI Pearl Crown Rayon	• Size 8 • 44 solid colors • 5 variegated colors	• Must be used in bobbin case that has been loosened. • Highly twisted, thicker rayon, threadlike cord that can be used in all quilts. • Use a longer stitch when machine quilting because of the thickness of thread. • Adds texture and sheen.
YLI Candlelight Textured Metallic Yarn	• Size 8 • 21 colors	• Must be used in bobbin case that has been loosened. • Great yarn for couching. • Use a longer stitch when machine quilting because of the thickness of thread. • Good for wall or lap quilts. • A personal favorite, adds glitz and glitter to projects.
YLI Shimmer Thread	• Size 8 • 15 solid colors • Rayon yarn twisted with a bit of metallic.	• Must be used in bobbin case that has been loosened. • Great yarn for couching. • Use a longer stitch when machine quilting because of the thickness of thread. • Good for wall or lap quilts.

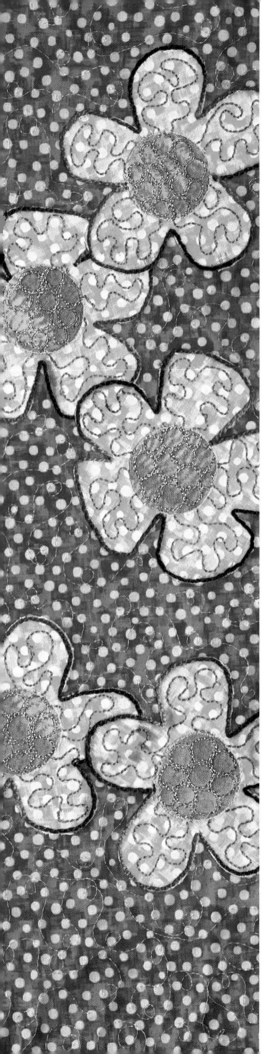

Fusing Basics

✿ ✿ ✿ ✿ ✿

Fusing is a fast fabulous "quicksew" way to appliqué shapes and other cool stuff onto your quilts! Simply put, you draw your image on the fusible product, iron it to the back of fabric, cut it out, then iron it to the quilt top. *Viola!* You're done. Now, isn't that so much easier than pesky needle-turn appliqué? I sure think so! Included in the book are great project ideas that have tons of fusing in them. When we combine this appliqué and bobbin work, you're sure to have a quilt that's a stunner!

The process of fusing is a simple one, but there are lots of products and things you need to know before proceeding, so let's begin!

Fusible Web Basics

Fusible web is a man-made fiber that melts when heated. When it is put between two pieces of fabric and ironed, it melts and fuses the two fabrics together. There are many kinds of fusible web on the market. You can buy it in rolls, in prepackaged pieces, and off a bolt. It also comes in very thin widths, but for what we do in the book, you need a full width (usually 22" to 45", depending on the brand).

The supply list for each project will specify an amount along with the number of square inches needed, so you can figure how much to get of whatever width is available to you. If the fusible is not large enough for the area being fused, you can butt pieces together.

The table on page 30 outlines the most popular types and for what each is best suited. Your project dictates which type of fusible

Fusing Basics ✿ ✿ ✿ ✿ ✿ ✿ ✿

Most Popular Fusibles	
Fusible	**Description/Things to Know**
Shades Soft Fuse™ Fusible Web by Stacy Michell	• Paper-backed and incredibly lightweight; you can layer and sew up to 4 pieces. • Because of how soft and lightweight it is, you can use it with a variety of fabrics. • Must be sewn down.
Mistyfuse™ Web	• Its paperless method allows you to use the traced image, so there is no need to reverse. If you choose to use this fusible for the book projects, you will need to use a reverse image since the templates are drawn for those using paper-backed fusible • Good for all weights of fabric from velvets and cottons to delicate tulles and organza. • Handles well, is incredibly sheer, doesn't add bulk to your fused piece. • Must be sewn down.
Pellon® Wonder-Under® Fusible Web	• Medium-weight fusible web with paper backing. • Must be sewn down. • Cannot layer too many pieces or it will get stiff and difficult to sew through.
Pellon® Wonder-Under® Heavy Duty	• Paper-backed and double the adhesive; great for wearable or home decor projects where extra adhesive is needed. • Cannot be sewn down.
Lite Steam-A-Seam® Iron-on Fusible Web	• Paper-backed lightweight fusible web. • Like the original Steam-A-Seam. Has a pressure-sensitive adhesive that allows for a temporary hold to your materials, but lighter. Allows you to layer more pieces with less stiffness. • Must be sewn down.
Lite Steam-A-Seam 2® Double Stick Fusible Web	• Similar to Lite Steam-a-Seam, but has a "sticky" back. You can hold your project vertically and the appliqué pieces stay in place and are still repositionable until fused with an iron. • Must be sewn down.
Heatnbond® Lite Iron-on Adhesive	• Paper-backed web that has the strongest bonding power of all the lightweight adhesives. • Cannot layer too many pieces or they will get stiff and difficult to sew through. • Must be sewn down, although it will stay bonded for a while without being sewn. • Can sew down, but only on the edges. If you try to machine quilt the inside of your fused piece, needle will get gummed up.
Heatnbond® Ultra Hold	• Paper-backed web whose bond is extremely strong. It's 3 times stronger than any other traditional web. • Can be used with a wide range of fabric. • Perfect choice for projects that you do not want to sew because the bond is super-strong and the edges do not need to be sealed. • Can't be sewn. This fuse is too heavy and it will gum up your needle.

bobbin **QUILTIN'** & fusin' **FUN** ✿ MICHELE SCOTT

web you should use. For the projects in the book, I use Shades Soft Fuse Fusible Web. It is my personal favorite because of the soft drape it provides.

I often layer my fused pieces and sew through them. For this, I need a very lightweight fusible. If it's too thick, the piece will be stiff and sewing through it will be an exercise in futility with broken threads and bent and gummed needles. But like anything, you have to find your own personal favorite. Use the chart as a stepping off point. Experiment with a variety of fusibles and choose the one that's best for you.

Bits of Fusing Wisdom

- There are two sides to fusible web—the paper side and the web (glue) side. NEVER iron the "web" side that has the fusible on it. It will destroy your iron.

- Are you going to sew over that fused piece to secure it? If not, you need to use a heavyweight fusible. And if you use the heavyweight fusible, you CAN NOT sew through it. The web is too heavy and it will dull and gum up your needle. For the projects in this book we sew every fused piece, so it is essential that you use the lightweight fusible web.

- When choosing a fusible for your project, think carefully. If you are layering a lot of pieces, the fuse must be lightweight or the project will be stiff and not pliable. This is the reason why Soft Fuse is my first choice. It keeps the project soft.

- No matter which fusible web you choose, be sure to read and follow the manufacturer's directions thoroughly. Different brands require different heat settings. Never assume they're all the same!

- Always test the fusible first. You never know how your particular material is going to react to the web. I once had a nightmare experience when the paper would not peel from the fabric. This was after I had already traced the necessary 120 petals for the flowers. In short, the fabric was of poor quality and the fusible bonded with the paper. I had to start from scratch. Ten minutes of testing can save you hours of frustration!

- Always use an appliqué sheet on your ironing surface when pressing fusible to your fabric. An appliqué sheet is a double-sided sheet made from an ultra high-temperature fabric that is coated with a non-stick treatment. If some of the web is peeking out of the fabric, it will protect your ironing board. Once you get that web stuff on your ironing board, it's a mess. Best to have a sheet to protect the board.

- Invest in a very cheap iron or pick one up at your local thrift shop. Mark it and use it as your fusing iron (Fig. 2–1, page 32). I don't trust myself not to goof up! As careful as you think you may be, there are times you may iron directly on the web and gum up your iron. Keep some heat-activated iron cleaner on hand.

Fusing Basics ✿ ✿ ✿ ✿ ✿ ✿ ✿

Fig. 2–1

Fig. 2–2

Fig. 2–3

Fig. 2–4

❤ Remember that your traced image is going on the BACK of your fabric, so you need to trace the reversed image. I trace my images with a dark permanent marker on a piece of thin paper. You can use regular old computer paper, but tracing paper or Golden Threads Quilting Paper work best. When you turn the paper over, the tracing has bled through and the reversed image is ready. *NOTE: All the patterns in the book are reverse image, so no worries there!*

Let's Fuse It!

Let's give it a try with my favorite image, a flower!

1. Place the fusible web, paper side up, glue side down on top of the image to be traced. Trace the image on the paper side of the web (Fig. 2–2).

The web is usually so light, it is easy to see the image under it. If it's a problem, you can darken the template with a thick black marker. If you have a variety of shapes, it's important to label each design as you trace.

2. Loosely cut the shapes apart, being sure to leave at least ¼" around each of the shapes.

3. Position the shape on the back of the desired fabric, glue side toward the fabric and paper toward the iron (Fig. 2–3).

4. Following the manufacturer's instructions, iron the fusible onto the fabric. Be sure that the appliqué is flat and in the perfect position before fusing.

5. Cut the design along the traced lines with sharp scissors. (Fig. 2–4).

6. Remove the paper backing from the appliqué (Fig. 2–5, page 33).

bobbin **QUILTIN'** & fusin' **FUN** ✿ MICHELE SCOTT

7. Position the appliqué on the background fabric, glue side down. Press with a hot iron to fuse your appliqué (Fig. 2–6).

Depending on the type of fusible, you may need to stitch it down. All of my projects have some type of quilting on the appliqués. I prefer to use the lightweight fusibles and I think the quilting adds interest to the project. All of the quilting designs I used are in the My Favorite Doodles section (pages 24–25).

That's it! It really is that easy!

Tips to Make Your Fusing Quicker and Easier!

- ◉ Finding that edge to separate the paper from the fabric can sometimes prove difficult. If the paper doesn't easily come off, score the back with a seam ripper and the paper should come right off (Fig. 2–7).

- ◉ Having sharp scissors to cut out your fused pieces is essential to a nice clean edge. I highly recommend Clover® Patchwork Scissors. They have fine teeth finishing to prevent fabric slippage. A finely serrated blade firmly grabs fabric and enables precise cutting as well as clean-cut edges for multi-layer cutting, including layers of fusing.

- ◉ If your fused pieces start coming off of the background, you can use a couple of drops of basting glue to secure them. If you don't have any glue on hand, a fine thin pin will suffice.

- ◉ Doing a project with a lot of the same pieces? There are a couple of ways to cut multiple pieces. The easiest is to invest in an AccuQuilt® GO!® Fabric Cutting system (see Resources, page 94). They have tons of dies to easily cut layers of fabric and a lot of appliqué pieces at one time (with the fusible web on the back!). I cut 180 flower petals for GARDEN OF HAPPINESS in no time at all. I didn't even have to trace ahead of time. You just iron the fusible on the back of your fabric and roll the fabric through the system.

Fig. 2–5

Fig. 2–6

Fig. 2–7

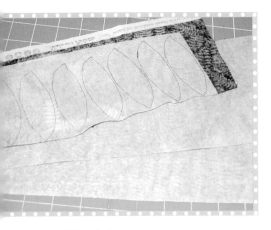

Fig. 2–8

Fig. 2–9

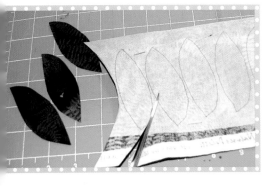

Fig. 2–10

Fig. 2–11

◉ A less expensive way to cut multiple pieces was suggested to me by a friend...and I love it. Tɪᴘᴛᴏᴇ Tʜʀᴏᴜɢʜ ᴛʜᴇ Tᴜ-ʟɪᴘs required a lot of the same shapes. Here's how to do it.

1. Trace a line of the petals on a strip of fusible web. Using the same size as that strip, iron two blank fusible web strips onto fabric (Fig. 2–8).

2. Staple the three strips together outside of the drawn lines (Fig. 2–9).

3. Using nice sharp scissors, cut through all three layers. You get three for the price of one (Fig. 2–10)!

❤ If perfect circles are required, use a rotary circle cutter, available from Olfa, Clover, and Dritz (see Resources, page 94). (Fig. 2–11)

❤ If a wavy edge is required, either cut one freehand, use the Quilter's Wave Edge ruler (see Resources, page 94), or make a template to follow.

Tɪᴘᴛᴏᴇ Tʜʀᴏᴜɢʜ ᴛʜᴇ Tᴜʟɪᴘs, detail. Full quilt on page 57.

bobbin **QUILTIN**' & fusin' **FUN** ✿ MICHELE SCOTT

Projects

A Day at the Beach, 40" x 32", made by the author

A DAY AT THE BEACH

One of my favorite places in the world is the beach. No matter if it is the New Jersey Shore, Florida Gulf, Pacific Ocean, or the Caribbean, I enjoy sitting, watching the water, and reading a good book. The beach is the perfect subject for me!

The instructions for this project are the most detailed, which should help you better understand the construction process for all the projects.

Yardage

- Strips of light blue (sky), darker blue (ocean), and light brown (sand) fabric: 12" x 36" each
- Contrasting sea fabric: fat quarter (This fabric should be several shades lighter and brighter than the base ocean fabric so there is a clear contrast between the two.)
- Solid black: ⅜ yard
- Binding: ½ yard (*I used the same variegated fabric as the flowers.*)
- Variety of fat eighths for the sun, umbrella, chairs, and flowers
- Backing: 42" x 34"

Other Supplies

- Batting: 42" x 34"
- Fusible web: total of 45" x 36" (1,620 square inches)
- Piece of tulle or cheesecloth to match ocean fabric: 14" x 40"
- Assortment of threads/yarns
- Invisible thread
- Pinking rotary cutter (optional, but fun!)
- The Wave Edge™ Ruler (optional)

Preparing the Background

1. Iron 2" strips of fusible web on both long edges on the back of the 12" x 36" ocean fabric. If the fusible is not long enough, you can butt pieces together. Using a rotary cutter, cut small waves on one long edge of the piece and large waves on the opposite edge. I used the Wave Edge ruler, but you could cut the waves freehand or make a paper template to follow (Fig. 3–1).

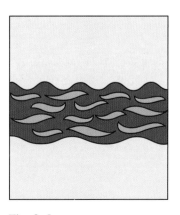

Fig. 3–1

2. Position the ocean fabric on top of the sand and sky. Carefully measure to ensure the measurement from the top to the bottom edge is equal along the left and right sides and through the middle. (It will be about 26".) Protect your ironing surface with an appliqué sheet (see page 31) and fuse the fabrics together.

3. Layer the background with the batting and backing. The batting and backing should extend at least 5" beyond the background. You will fuse the border on top of the prepared background later.

Let's Make Waves!

The ocean is not a flat, static surface. It always has waves and whitecaps. I wanted to add some of that action.

1. Iron fusible web onto the back of the fat quarter of contrasting ocean fabric. Draw a set of freeform wave designs with a pencil (Fig. 3–2). Have fun with this as you draw a variety of sizes and curves. Cut out the waves on the drawn lines and fuse to the base ocean fabric.

2. Place cheesecloth or tulle over the entire ocean area. Do not be concerned if it covers the sky and sand a bit. Using monofilament thread, free-motion quilt along the wavy lines at the top and bottom of the ocean to secure the tulle. Carefully cut away the excess.

3. Make the ocean sparkle by quilting it with silver flat polyester film (see the thread chart, pages 27–28). If you use it in the needle, use a vertical spool holder. It's a film, not a thread, and it will twist and break if it comes off a horizontal spool. If you are bobbin quilting the ocean, use the free-motion wave lines to see your area. I did a simple allover meander (Fig. 3-3).

4. Couch yarn over the raw edges of the top and the bottom edges of the fused ocean.

Fig. 3–3

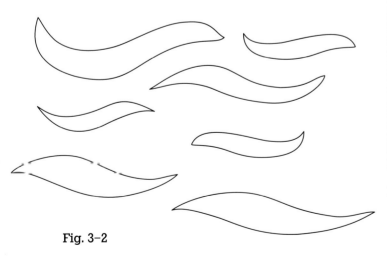

Fig. 3–2

Sun in the Sky: Creating a Single Unit

I love using swirls, so I used one for the center of my sun. Triangles for the rays complete it.

1. Trace the sun templates (8 rays, one swirl, page 42) onto fusible web. Fuse the swirl and rays to the BACK of the yellow sun fabric and cut out. Fuse the sun pieces onto the FRONT of a piece of black fabric (Fig. 3-4).

2. Fuse a piece of web to the back of the black fabric with the sun on the front. Be sure that it extends beyond all of the sun pieces (Fig. 3-5).

3. Using a rotary ruler as a guide, trim with a wavy cutter to leave a small margin of black around all the outer edges of the sun (Fig. 3-6).

4. Fuse to the right side of the sky. The black outline gives the sun sharp definition while the waves remind me of the wavy lines heat makes on a hot summer day.

5. With a gold metallic thread, machine quilt a zigzag stitch around the edges of the yellow fabric. Finish off the area by quilting the sky with swirls and points with rayon thread (Fig. 3-7).

To the Beach!

1. Trace and fuse the blanket in the same manner as the sun, with the black behind it. Place an assortment of yarns at each end under the blanket to simulate fringe. Secure the yarn in place with pins.

2. Trace and fuse the one-piece umbrella shape of black fabric; trace and fuse the umbrella panels. Position the panels on the umbrella and fuse in place.

Fig. 3–4

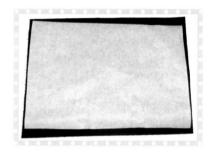

Fig. 3–5

Fig. 3–6

Fig. 3–7

Fig. 3–8

3. Arrange the umbrella, beach blanket, and chairs on the sand and fuse in place. Quilt a decorative design on the umbrella panels with variegated rayon thread. Finish the umbrella by couching a gold metallic cord around each of the colored sections. Fill in black areas with black metallic thread using a free-motion zigzag stitch (Fig. 3-8).

4. Using the same variegated rayon thread as on the umbrella, quilt circles on the blanket. The color changes worked out almost perfectly to be in each circle that made it look like a printed design. Never underestimate serendipity! Add a red satin stitch to outline the blanket. It will hold the blanket and fringe down. Fill in black areas with black metallic thread using a free-motion zigzag stitch (Fig. 3-9).

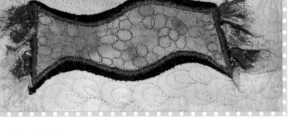

Fig. 3–9

5. Trace the outline of the beach chairs and fuse to the back of black fabric. Trace the chair back and seat pieces (parallelograms and triangles) and fuse to the backs of the different color fabrics. Cut out all the pieces on the drawn lines. Fuse the backs and seats to the chairs.

6. Free-motion zigzag stitch with matching rayon to the chair backs. Fill in black areas with black metallic thread using a free-motion zigzag stitch (Fig. 3-10).

7. Finish by machine quilting a feather pattern over the sand with matching rayon thread.

Fig. 3–10

Finishing Up!

1. Cut 2" strips of lightweight fusible web and 5" x width-of-fabric strips of black. Iron the fusible web along the edge of the back side of the black.

2. Use a pinking cutter and a ruler to pink the edge along the fused web.

3. Carefully "square" the finished top, being sure it is a rectangle. Draw pencil lines on the background where the border will go to ensure accuracy. Fuse the borders one at a time, overlapping each border strip with the one applied previously.

4. After fusing the borders, peel back the top layer of the overlap in each corner and cut off the excess bottom layer.

5. Secure the borders permanently by couching a decorative yarn right next to the pinked edge. Always start the yarn couching under the border. Tack the end of the yarn with your zigzag stitch and then zigzag down the rest of the yarn. When you bring the other border on top of the one you are working on, the yarn edge will be covered.

6. Trace 13 flower templates (page 43) on fusible web and iron to the back of the fabric of your choice. I chose a variegated fabric for this piece so that every flower was a different color and followed a progression—very dramatic on the black. Place the flowers in the border around the top left corner of the piece and fuse in place (Fig. 3-11).

7. Machine quilt rectangular fingers around the border, which will secure the appliquéd flowers. I used a thicker thread (size 12) for the border and variegated cotton thread to tie in with the multicolored flowers. You can use it through the needle or in the bobbin (if the needle technique is not behaving, as it wasn't for me). I quilted from the back. I knew where the border ended because of the couching that I had done. I used black thread in the needle so if I had any tension issues, it would not be visible on the quilt top.

8. Cut 2¼" strips for the binding and bind the quilt.

Fig. 3–11

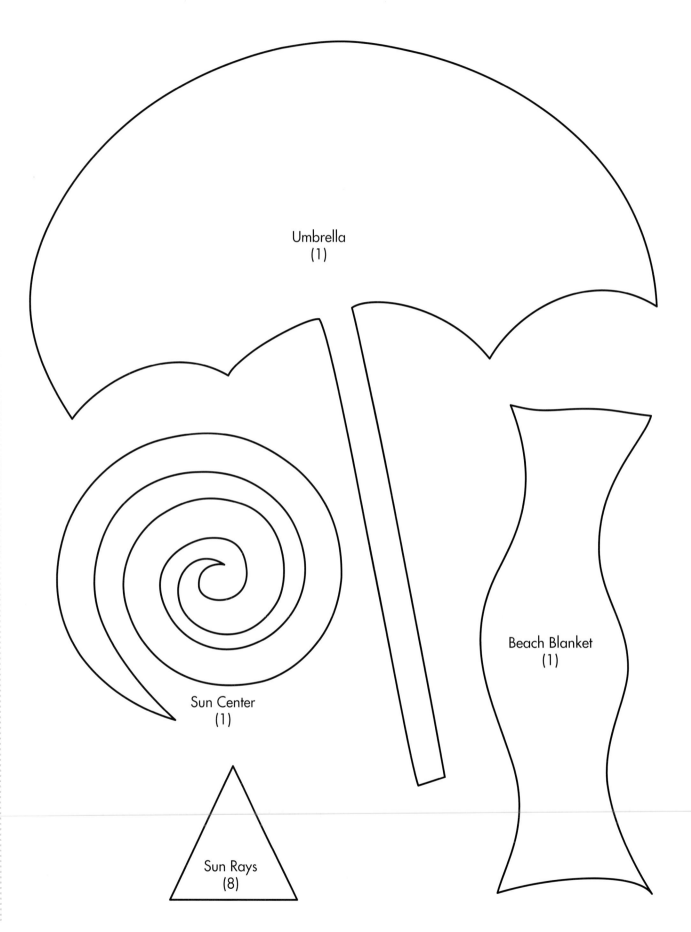

Umbrella
(1)

Sun Center
(1)

Sun Rays
(8)

Beach Blanket
(1)

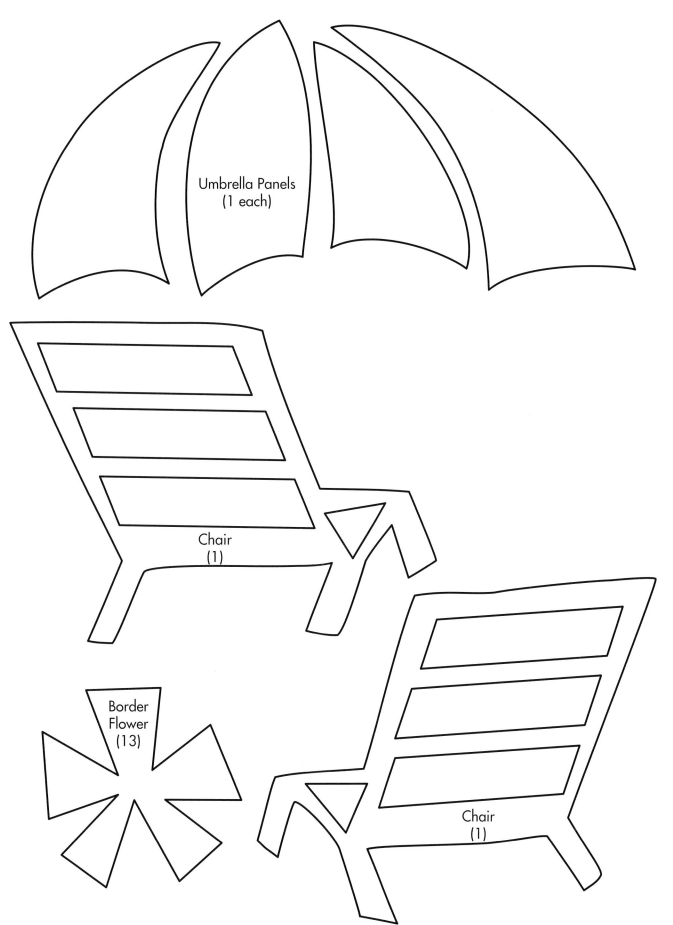

Umbrella Panels
(1 each)

Chair
(1)

Border
Flower
(13)

Chair
(1)

GARDEN OF HAPPINESS, 56" x 68", pieced by Elinore Locke, quilted by the author

GARDEN OF HAPPINESS

✿ ✿ ✿ ✿ ✿

This is my favorite quilt in the book! Flowers in general make me happy, as you can easily tell from my projects! I call it GARDEN OF HAPPINESS because this quilt brings me so much happiness during the cold, dark winter months. I used my Nature's Palette collection from Northcott silk for this quilt, but any great tonal fabrics would look good!

As you begin piecing the top you will notice that we don't fuse the flowers until the end. Sometimes when using lightweight fusible, the fused fabric may detach from the top, especially if you are manipulating the fabric a lot. Whenever I have a larger project with a lot of fusing, I wait to fuse until I'm ready to quilt.

You may also notice that you have a border strip that is not included in the sample quilt. There is a simple explanation for this—I messed up. I sent my mother home with fabric and directions on how to piece the top. The directions were wrong but my goodness, she made it work! The poor woman stretched and skewed things to make that border fit without those extra strips. We can assure you that the extra strip is necessary, and you won't have the issues my poor mom did!

Yardage
- Background fabric (light green): 1½ yards
- Flower centers (light yellow): ⅓ yard
- Blocks/quilt squares: an assortment of 9 tonal fabrics, a total of 4 yards (I used green, light green, purple, light purple, red, blue, orange, light orange, and yellow.)
- Inner border/binding (dark blue): ¾ yard
- Backing: 3¼ yards

Other Supplies
- Batting: Twin
- Fusible web: total of 40" x 45" (1,800 square inches)
- Medium green ⅝" jumbo rickrack: 1 yard
- Assortment of decorative threads/yarns
- Invisible thread

Cutting Instructions

From the background fabric, cut:

- Five 12½" x 12½" squares
- Eleven 6½" x 6½" squares
- Four 6½" x 12½" rectangles

From the assortment of tonal fabrics, cut:

- Ninety-six 3½" x 3½" squares
  (for the eight-patch units)
- Thirty-six 5½" x 5½" squares
  (for the border blocks)
- Thirty-six 1½" x 5½" rectangles
  (for the border blocks)
- Thirty-six 1½" x 6½" rectangles
  (for the border blocks)

From the inner border/binding fabric, cut:

- Five 1½" x width-of-fabric strips
  (for the inner border)
- Seven 2¼" x width-of-fabric strips
  (for the binding)

Trace and Fuse

FLOWER PETALS

**Cut in sets of 5 per color (unless you
prefer a scrappier look).**

- 5 sets of Large Petal A (25 total)
- 11 sets of Medium Petal B (55 total)
- 36 sets of Border Petal C (180 total)
- 4 sets of Small Petal D (20 total)

Flower Centers (light yellow)

- 5 Large Center A
- 11 Medium Center B
- 36 Border Center C
- 4 Small Center D

Flower Leaves (green)

- 2 Leaf A
- 2 Leaf B

*Note: You can use Accuquilt template #55008/
Feathers for the small petals. I cut tons and tons
of them perfectly in no time! I cut the circles with
the Olfa® Rotary Circle Cutter.*

Piecing the Top

Piece the colors randomly. Don't get too hung
up on which colors go where. Just grab squares
and strips as you go, distributing them evenly. If
a color ends up next to itself, it's fine. This quilt
is so scrappy, you'll never know the difference.

1. Using the ninety-six 3½" x 3½" tonal
squares, sew 12 eight-patch units (Fig. 4–1).

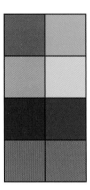

Fig. 4–1. Make 12 eight-patch units

2. Assemble the top in 7 sections using the
background blocks and eight-patch units. Join
the sections to complete the center of the top
(Fig. 4–2, page 47).

3. Piece the 1½" blue strips as needed. Cut 2 side borders 54½" and top and bottom borders 44½". Add to the quilt top.

4. Sew a 1½" x 5½" strip to the side of each of the thirty-six 5½" x 5½" square and press. Sew a different color 1½" x 6½" rectangle to an adjacent side of each block. Press. Make 36 (Fig. 4–3).

5. Make 4 border units of 9 blocks each, alternating the orientation of the blocks as desired.

6. Add 2 border units to the sides. Press toward the inner border. Add the remaining 2 border units to the top and bottom. Press as before.

7. Layer and baste to the batting and backing in preparation for fusing and finishing.

The Fun Part!

Apply the flowers and machine quilt approximately one-quarter of the quilt at a time. Do as much or as little at once as you are comfortable with. Press your quilt thoroughly after each section is quilted and complete.

1. Position petals, flower centers, leaves, and a rickrack stem. Since rickrack does not have fusible on the back, pin it in place. Be sure to tuck the ends of each rickrack stem under the leaf and petal.

2. Fuse the pieces in place.

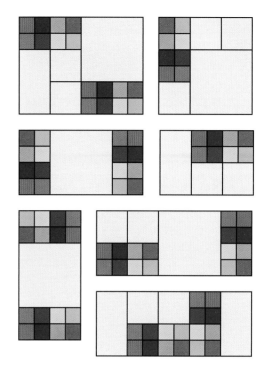

Fig. 4–2. Background assembly

Fig. 4–3. Make 36

Fig. 4–6

Fig. 4–6

Fig. 4–6

3. Prepare your machine for free-motion quilting with invisible thread in the top and whatever color you prefer in the bobbin. When you bobbin quilt this, you will be using the thread on the back as a guide, so if you want a clear and distinct line to follow, use a bobbin thread that contrasts with your backing fabric.

4. Starting from the point closest to the middle, free-motion a loop-de-loop all over the top. When you get to the flowers in the main section of the top, quilt just outside both the petals and centers. Don't stress if your quilting crosses. I promise it will be all right (Fig. 4–4)!

5. Secure the rickrack stem with a single free-motion stitch down its center.

6. As you get to the border flowers, quilt a swirl in the center, then just inside of the petals. We won't be bobbin quilting these flowers, so we need to secure them with sewing. After sewing the flower, outline it and then go on with your loop-de-loop quilting. Continue in this manner until you have appliquéd and quilted all of the flowers on the quilt (Fig. 4–5).

7. Wind the bobbin with thread for your petals and centers. I used YLI Candlelight that matched the top fabric. Use any thread in the top that matches the bobbin thread color. I chose to use invisible thread so I would not have to change my top thread every time I changed the bobbin color.

8. Turn the quilt over and bobbin quilt your flowers. I did a circle design in the centers and feather quilting on the petals (Fig. 4–6).

9. Repeat these steps to complete your quilt.

10. Bind with the 2¼" dark blue strips.

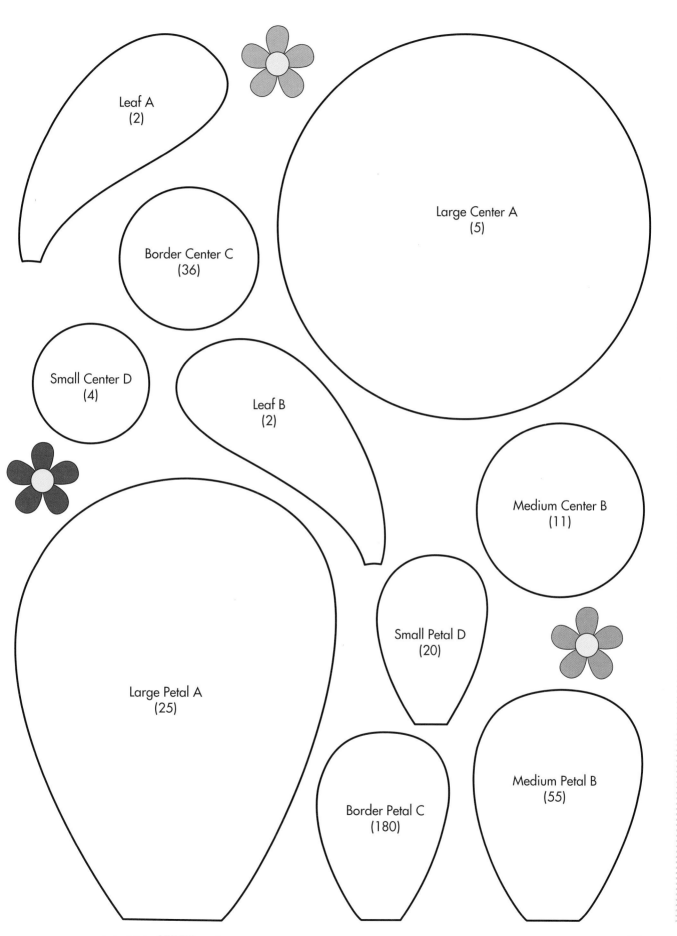

Leaf A
(2)

Border Center C
(36)

Large Center A
(5)

Small Center D
(4)

Leaf B
(2)

Medium Center B
(11)

Large Petal A
(25)

Small Petal D
(20)

Medium Petal B
(55)

Border Petal C
(180)

WILLOW TREE, 48" x 57", made by the author

WILLOW TREE

❀ ✿ ❀ ✿ ❀ ✿ ❀

What a wonderful way to showcase your stash! This is a surprisingly easy quilt that is quite a beauty. The border is especially lovely with a large assortment of fabrics from Northcott Silk.

- Tree/inner border (brown tonal): ¾ yard
- Binding (black tonal): ½ yard
- Backing: 3 yards

Yardage

- Border fabric (assortment of medium to dark tonals or batiks): 1⅛ yards total
- Tree leaves (same fabrics as border or something that coordinates): ⅔ yard total
- Background fabric (assortment of light tonals or batiks): 1¾ yards total

Other Supplies

- Batting: Twin or 56" x 66"
- Fusible web: total of 45" x 45" (2,025 square inches)
- Thick decorative brown yarn: 7 yards
- Assortment of decorative threads/yarns
- Invisible thread

Cutting Instructions

ROTARY CUTTING

From the assorted background fabrics, cut and label these rectangles.

# of Patches	Size	# of Patches	Size	# of Patches	Size
1 A	1½" x 4½"	1 M	4½" x 7½"	1 Y	5" x 6"
1 B	1½" x 5½"	2 N	3½" x 5½"	6 Z	5½" x 5½"
1 C	1½" x 9½"	3 O	4½" x 5½"	1 AA	5½" x 6"
1 D	2" x 5"	1 P	4½" x 8½"	4 BB	5½" x 6½"
1 E	2" x 7½"	2 Q	3½" x 9½"	3 CC	5½" x 7½"
1 F	2½" x 4½"	1 R	4" x 6½"	1 DD	5½" x 8½"
2 G	2½" x 6½"	1 S	4½" x 6½"	2 EE	5½" x 9½"
3 H	2½" x 7½"	1 T	4½" x 9½"	3 FF	6½" x 7½"
1 I	3" x 6 ½"	1 U	4½" x 12½"	1 GG	7½" x 8½"
1 J	3" x 9½"	1 V	5" x 5½"	2 HH	6½" x 9½"
5 K	3½" x 4½"	1 W	5" x 9½"		
5 L	4½" x 4½"	2 X	5" x 10½"		

From assorted medium/dark border fabrics, cut:
- One hundred and forty-eight 2" x 4½" rectangles

From the inner border fabric, cut:
- Five 1½" x width-of-fabric strips

From the black tonal, cut:
- Six 2¼" x width-of-fabric strips for the binding

Trace and Fuse
- 92 Leaf A (assorted medium/dark)
- Tree Templates B-K (brown)

Templates are the reverse of the tree picture, so when you trace, iron, cut, and fuse, the image will be as shown in the picture.

Piecing the Top

1. Lay out the background squares and rectangles as shown in the background assembly diagram. Join into sections and join the sections to complete the quilt center (Fig. 5–1, page 53).

2. Piece the inner border strips as needed and add to the sides and top and bottom of the quilt. The top should measure 38½" x 47½".

3. Sew two border units with forty 2" x 4½" assorted rectangles. Sew two border units with thirty-four assorted rectangles (Fig. 5–2, page 53). *(These are longer than the sides to allow for mitering the border corners.)*

4. Sew the borders to the sides, top, and bottom of the quilt, mitering the corners (Fig. 5–3, page 54).

5. Layer the top with batting and backing in preparation for fusing and finishing.

The Fun Part!

1. Referring to the layout (page 54), place the tree on the background. Do not fuse. Pin in place. (You will fuse the tree after the leaves are sewn down.)

2. Lay out the leaves on the tree and fuse them to the background.

3. Using a thick decorative yarn (I used YLI Candlelight) and invisible thread, couch a matching yarn just inside the edges of each leaf.

4. Turn the quilt to the back. Prepare the machine with the same decorative couched yarn in the bobbin and invisible thread in the top.

5. From the back, follow the couching zigzag and machine quilt a vein through each leaf. Match each vein to the color you used for the edges.

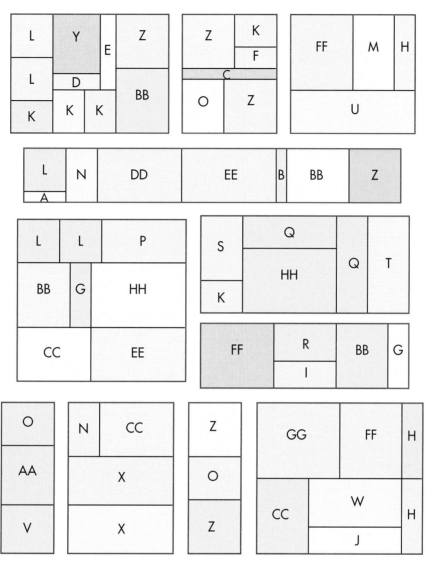

Fig. 5–1. Background layout

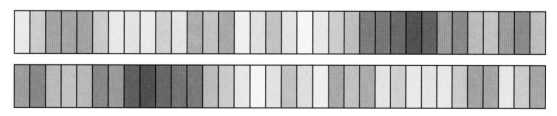

Make two sets of thirty-four 2" x 4½" rectangles.

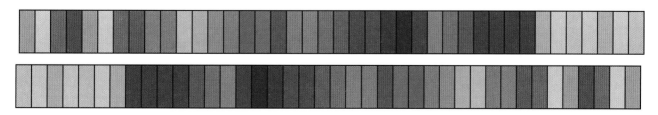

Make two sets of forty 2" x 4½" rectangles.

Fig. 5–2. Border units

6. Now that the leaves are sewn, turn quilt to the front and fuse the tree in place. Couch brown yarn along all the raw edges of the tree.

7. Turn the quilt to the back. Prepare your machine with a thick decorative thread in the bobbin that coordinates with the tree (I used YLI Candlelight Copper) and invisible thread in the top. Follow the couching zigzag on the back and machine quilt all through the tree.

8. Finish quilting in the way you see fit! For the pastel background, I used a size 12 variegated pastel cotton with swirls and points. I couched the same metallic yarn used for the tree in the seams of the inner border and finished with thin gold metallic feather quilting in the border.

9. Bind with the black tonal 2¼" strips.

Fig. 5–3. Border and tree layout

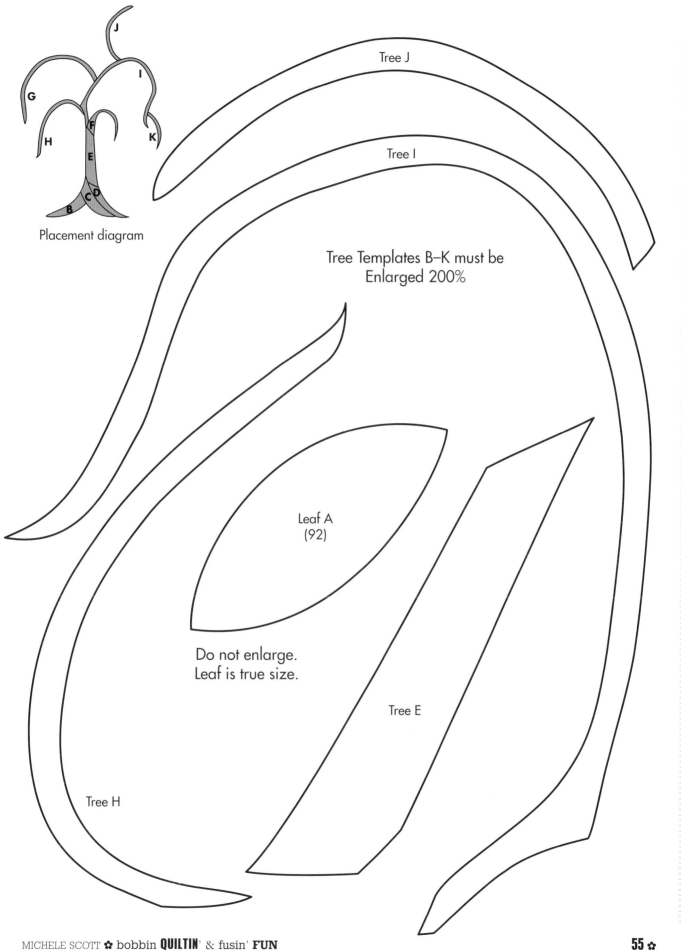

Placement diagram

Tree J

Tree I

Tree Templates B–K must be
Enlarged 200%

Leaf A
(92)

Do not enlarge.
Leaf is true size.

Tree E

Tree H

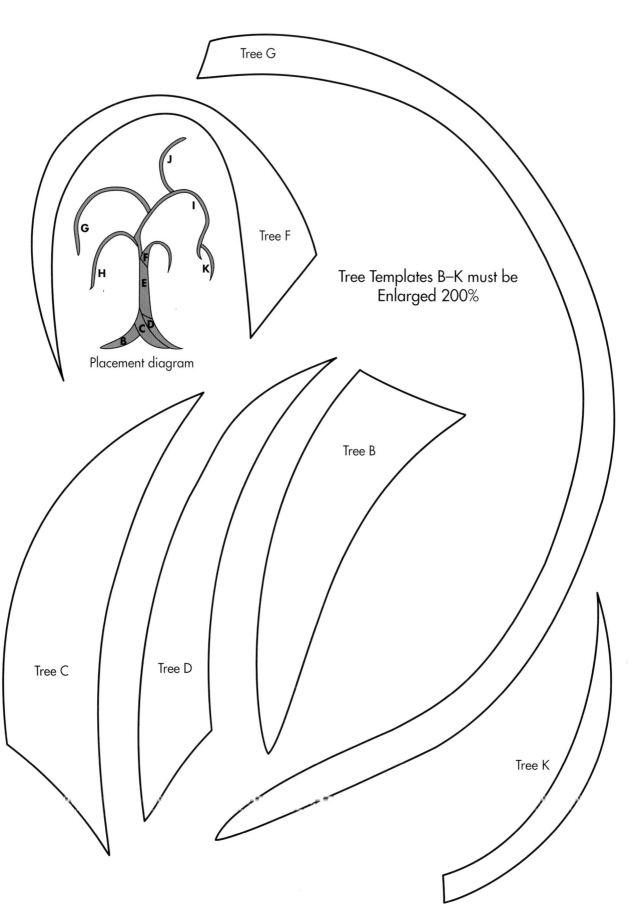

Tree G

Tree F

J

I

G

F

H

E

K

C D

B

Placement diagram

Tree Templates B–K must be
Enlarged 200%

Tree B

Tree C

Tree D

Tree K

TIPTOE THROUGH THE TULIPS, 64" x 64", made by the author

TIPTOE THROUGH THE TULIPS

✿ ✿ ✿ ✿ ✿

Spring is early and in bloom with these beautiful tulips! Didn't I tell you I loved flowers?

Yardage

- Background fabric: ¾ yard of each of 4 assorted light prints (3 yards total)
- Inside sashing/tulip stems (dark green): ¾ yard
- Outside sashing/border blocks/tulips/ binding (dark purple): 2 yards
- Border/tulip leaves (medium green): 1 yard
- Tulip centers (light purple): ¼ yard
- Backing: 4¼ yards

Other Supplies

- Batting: Twin or 72" x 72"
- Fusible web: total of 36" x 45" (1,620 square inches)
- Assortment of decorative threads/yarns
- Invisible thread

Cutting Instructions:

ROTARY CUTTING

From the background fabric, cut:
- Sixteen 12½" x 12½" squares

From the dark green sashing fabric, cut:
- Twelve 2" x 12½" strips
- Five 2" x width-of-fabric strips

From the dark purple, cut:
- Six 2¼" x width-of-fabric strips
- Four 4½" x 4½" squares
- Twenty-eight 4½" x 8½" rectangles
- Seven 2¼" strips for the binding

From the medium green border fabric, cut:
- Fifty-six 4½" x 4½" squares

Trace and Fuse

TULIPS
- 32 Leaf A (medium green)
- 32 Leaf B (medium green)
- 48 Petal C (dark purple)
- 48 Petal D (dark purple)
- 48 Center E (light purple)

STEMS – Iron fusible web to the back of the ¼ yard of dark green fabric. Cut:
- Sixteen ½" x 11" strips for stem H
- Thirty-two ½" x 5" strips for stems F and G

Piecing the Top

1. Fuse 11" and 5" stems onto the sixteen 12½" x 12½" background squares. Be sure the 5" side stems are under the 11" main stem. Trim the ends to square the block (Fig. 6–1).

2. Piece the 2" dark green strips as needed. Cut three 2" x 53" inner sashing strips.

3. Lay out the 16 background squares, twelve 2" x 12½" sashing strips, and three 2" x 53" sashing strips. Join the blocks and small strips into rows; join the rows and large strips together (Fig. 6–2).

4. Piece the 2¼" dark purple strips as needed. Cut two 2¼" x 53" inner borders and add them to the sides. Cut two 2¼" x 56½" inner borders and add them to the top and bottom.

5. Make 28 Flying Geese units as follows. Draw a diagonal line on the wrong side of the fifty-six green border 4½" x 4½" squares. Align a marked green square with one end of a purple 4½" x 8½" rectangle, right sides together. Sew directly on the drawn line, trim ¼" from the sewing line, and press the seam toward the purple. Repeat with a second square at the opposite end of the rectangle (Fig. 6–3, page 60).

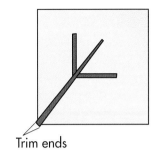

Trim ends

Fig. 6–1. Fusing the stems

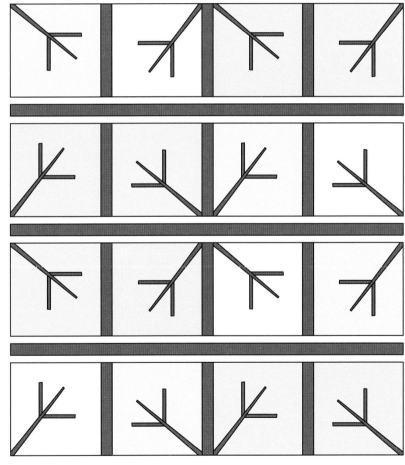

Fig. 6–2. Background layout

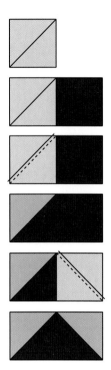

Fig. 6–3. Make 28 Flying Geese units.

In the interests of "going green," save the trimmed triangles to make a total of 56 half-square triangle units to use in another project.

6. Sew sets of seven Flying Geese units end-to-end. Make 4 sets. Sew 2 sets to the sides of the quilt. Add two 4½" x 4½" squares to the ends of the remaining sets and add to the top and bottom to complete the top (Fig. 6-4).

7. Layer with batting and backing in preparation for fusing and finishing.

The Fun Part!

1. Place and fuse the tulip centers, petals, and leaves to the background of the completed quilt top.

Fig. 6–4. Add inner and Flying Geese borders to the quilt top.

2. Use invisible thread in the top of the machine and in the bobbin. If you are not comfortable using invisible thread in the bobbin, use any cotton thread that matches the quilt backing. Machine quilt the entire top (I used swirls and points). Outline the whole tulip, stem, and leaf with the invisible thread as you free-motion quilt. These lines will be your guides when you bobbin quilt the tulips and leaves.

3. Turn the quilt to the back. Prepare the machine with a thick decorative thread of your choice in the bobbin (I used a matching YLI Pearl Rayon) and invisible thread in the top. Quilt the tulip petals with a curlicue meander and the leaves with zigzag free-motion stitch (Fig. 6-5).

4. Bind with the 2¼" dark purple strips.

Fig. 6–5. Bobbin quilting detail

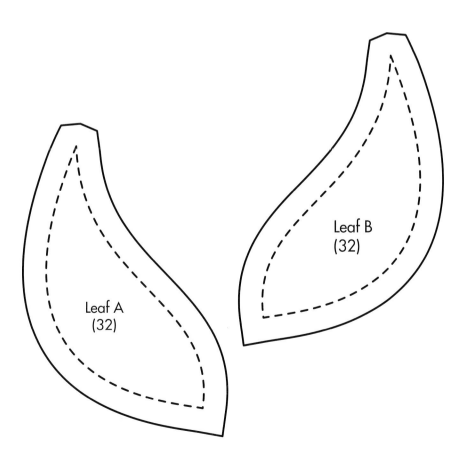

Leaf B
(32)

Leaf A
(32)

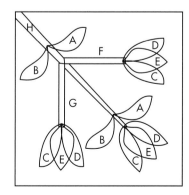

Placement diagram

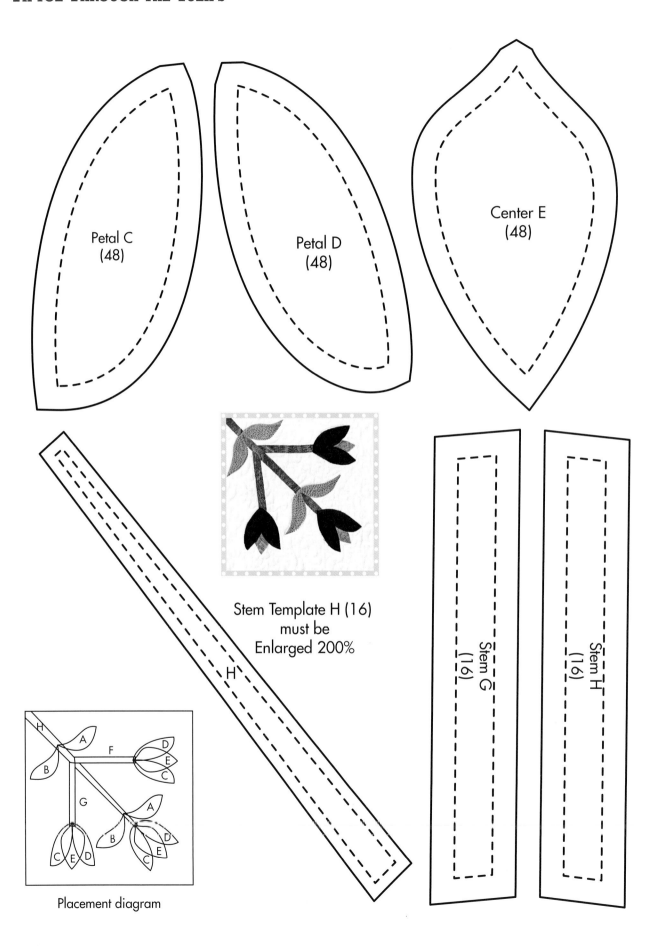

Petal C
(48)

Petal D
(48)

Center E
(48)

Stem Template H (16)
must be
Enlarged 200%

H

Stem G
(16)

Stem H
(16)

Placement diagram

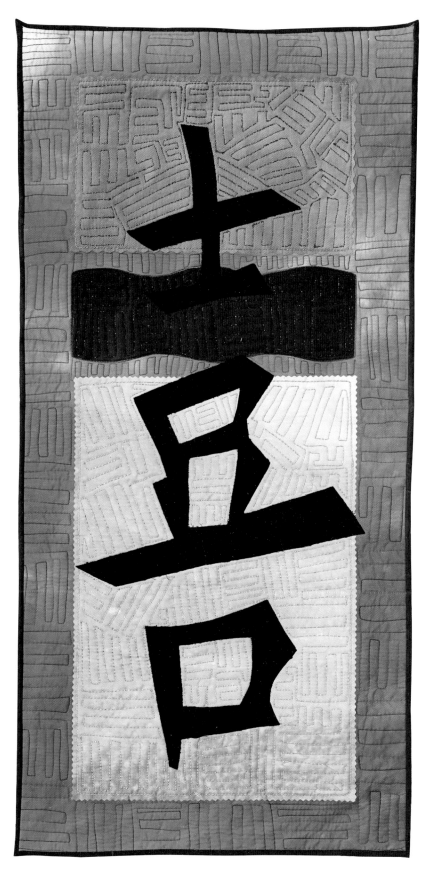

XI (HAPPINESS), 19½" x 41", made by the author

Xi (Happiness)

✿ ✿ ✿ ✿ ✿

When I recently met my husband, Tom, I experienced true happiness for the first time in a very long time. Quilters love to express themselves through our art, so I created this for him. His selfless love has taught me what true happiness is.

Yardage

- Solid black cotton: ½ yard
- Orange batik/dyed (top rectangle): 9" x 14"
- Dark blue batik/dyed (middle rectangle): 5" x 14"
- Lime green batik/dyed (bottom rectangle): 14" x 21"
- Medium blue batik/dyed (background): ½ yard, cut to 20" x 40"
- Backing: 20" x 42"

Other Supplies

- Batting: 20" x 42"
- Fusible web: 36" x 45" total (1,620 square inches)
- Assortment of decorative yarns and thread that coordinate with fabrics.
- Invisible thread
- Pinking and wavy blades for rotary cutter (optional)
- Wave Edge ruler (optional)

Creating Art!

1. Iron fusible web to the back of the three rectangles. You can leave them as is with no decorative threads, or you can cut each in a different manner as I did, or make up your own combination of edges.

2. Layer the background fabric with the batting and backing. Center the rectangles on the background so that there is approximately 3" extending around the top, bottom, and sides with 1½"–2" between each rectangle. Fuse the rectangles to the background.

3. Couch thick shimmery thread/yarn around each rectangle with invisible thread. (For the top and bottom rectangles, I couched hand-

-dyed cotton size 5 from Artfabrik with YLI Shimmer.) Couch JUST inside the pinked/waved/fused edges (Fig.7–1).

4. Enlarge the XI templates 200% (pages 66–67). Trace onto the fusible and iron to the back of the solid black. Cut out the shapes and place on top of the completed background using the picture as a guide. Don't mix them up or you're likely to make another Chinese word! Fuse to the background.

5. Using a thicker black thread on top and black in the bobbin, free-motion zigzag inside the symbols to secure them. Remember to fill in the areas while moving the piece up and down, not across, or you will get a straight line (Fig.7–2).

6. Wind a bobbin with thick thread (I used the YLI shimmer again). Turn the quilt over and bobbin quilt with the back and forth quilting design in each section. Match the thread color with the fabric in each section (Figs.7–3 and 7–4).

7. Finish the quilt by machine quilting a back and forth design in the background sections from the front or back. I did it from the front using a cotton variegated Artfabrik thread size 12. Square off the edges and bind with the remaining dark blue fabric.

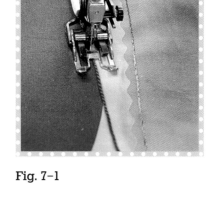

Fig. 7–1

Fig. 7–2

Fig. 7–3

Fig. 7–4

Don't mix them up or you're likely to make another Chinese word!

Middle symbol

Enlarge 200%
Cut (1) from black

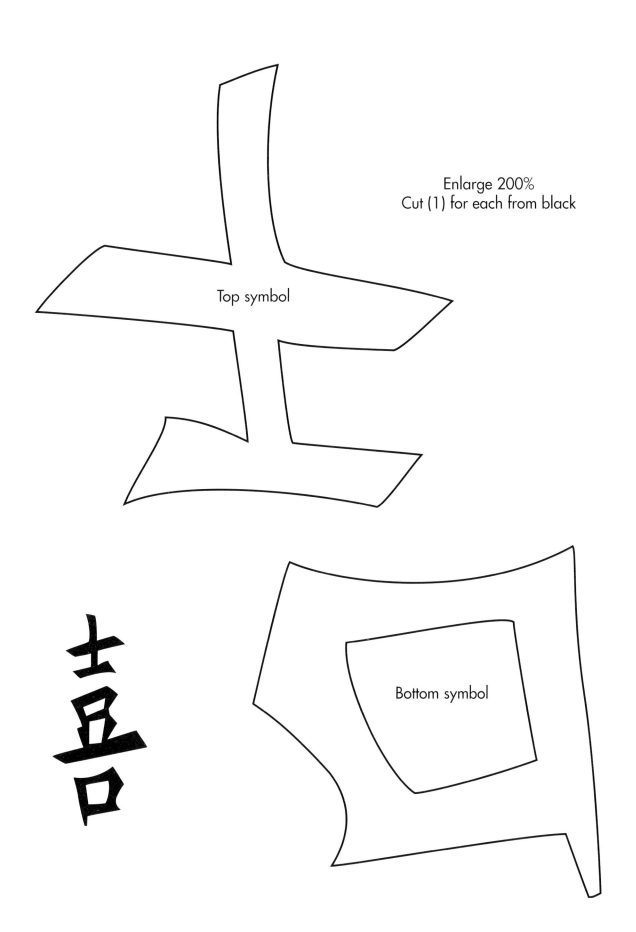

Enlarge 200%
Cut (1) for each from black

Top symbol

Bottom symbol

CIRCLE OF FRIENDS, 29" x 21", made by Cyndi Souder, Annandale, VA
(www.moonlightingquilts.com)

CIRCLE OF FRIENDS

✿ ✿ ✿ ✿ ✿

Cyndi Souder stretched out of her comfort zone during my fusing class to create a tribute to her sister and those friends of hers who rallied around during her fight with ovarian cancer. This beautiful and inspirational piece can be made with the gorgeous color purple or whatever fabrics you'd like to showcase for your own tribute.

Yardage

- 4 coordinating batiks—1 light, 1 medium, and 2 darks
    - Light: ⅜ yard
    - Medium: ⅜ yard
    - Dark #1: Fat quarter
    - Dark #2: ¼ yard
- Variety of medium and dark coordinating batik scraps for the "friends" and moon
- Binding: ¼ yard dark purple
- Backing: ⅝ yard

Other Supplies

- Batting: 32" x 24"
- Fusible web: Fat quarter (396 square inches)
- Assortment of decorative threads (Only one area will be bobbin quilted, so you can stick with the thinner cotton and rayon threads for this project.)

Cutting Instructions

From the light batik cut:
- One 10" x 24" rectangle (for the sky)

From the medium batik cut:
- One 10" x 24" rectangle (for the hill)

From Dark #1 cut:
- Two strips 4½" x 22" (for the side borders)

From Dark #2 cut:
- One 5" x 24" rectangle (for the top border)

From the binding fabric cut:
- Three 2¼" strips

From the backing cut:
- One piece 32" x 24"

Making the Top

1. Iron 3" strips of fusible web on one of the long edges of the 2 side borders, the top border, and the medium hill fabric.

2. Layer the batting on top of the backing.

3. Position the sky piece on the batting so that 4" of batting extends beyond the top and sides.

Fig. 8–1

Fig. 8–2

4. Free-form cut a hill shape along the fused edge of the medium fabric. Position the hill over the bottom edge of the sky. Fuse in place.

5. Free-form cut subtle waves along the fused edge of the top and side borders. Position at the top and sides of the hill and sky and fuse in place.

6. With invisible thread and a zigzag stitch, couch yarn on the lower raw edge of the top border. Couch a thicker variegated cord to the curved edge of the hill.

7. Trace and fuse the friends and moon templates (pages 72–73) to the assortment of batiks. Make 2 friend #4, one as shown and one in reverse. Cut from the fabric. Position the friends using the numbers as a guide. Position the moon to the top left-hand corner spanning the top border and background. When satisfied with the placement, fuse to the background.

The Fun Part!

1. Quilt the friends using an assortment of rayon threads and the shape of each body as a guide. Echo quilt some and free-motion zigzag the others. The quilting stitches add the impression of dimension (Fig. 8–1).

2. Quilt the sky using rayon thread and the print of the fabric as a guide to create misty cloud impressions (Fig. 8–2).

3. Quilt the moon with a combination of patterns (Fig. 8–3).

4. Quilt the hill with rayon thread following the pattern of the fabric and stippling in between the motifs (Fig. 8–4).

5. Bobbin quilt the top border with size 12 thread.

6. The side borders are the most impressive part about this piece. Cyndi quilted them from the top with QuiltWriting, a quilting technique she developed. The words are things that she and her sister said to each other. What a wonderful way to finish something so special (Fig. 8–5).

7. Square up and bind with the 2¼" strips.

Fig. 8–3

Fig. 8–4

Fig. 8–5

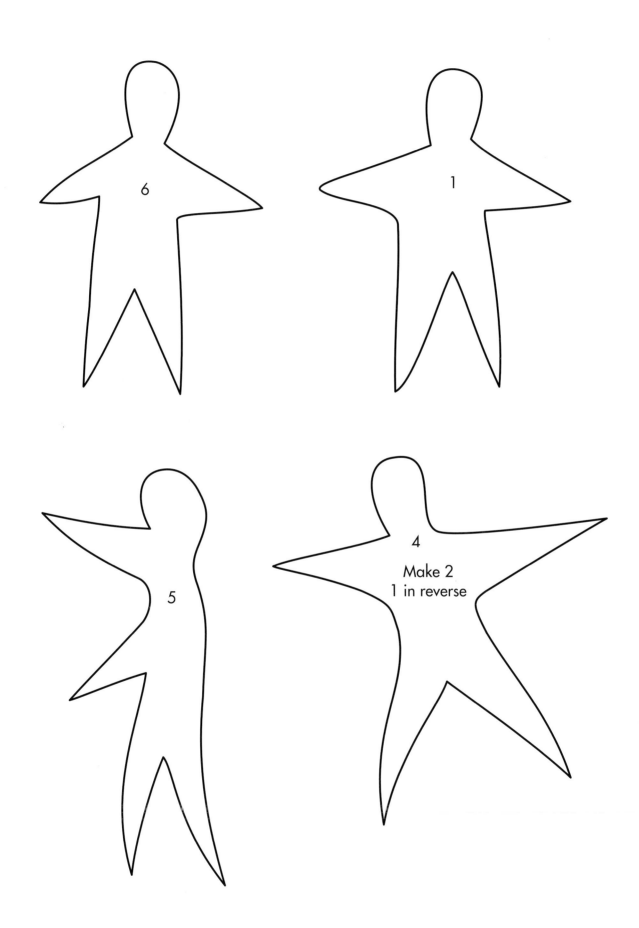

6

1

5

4

Make 2
1 in reverse

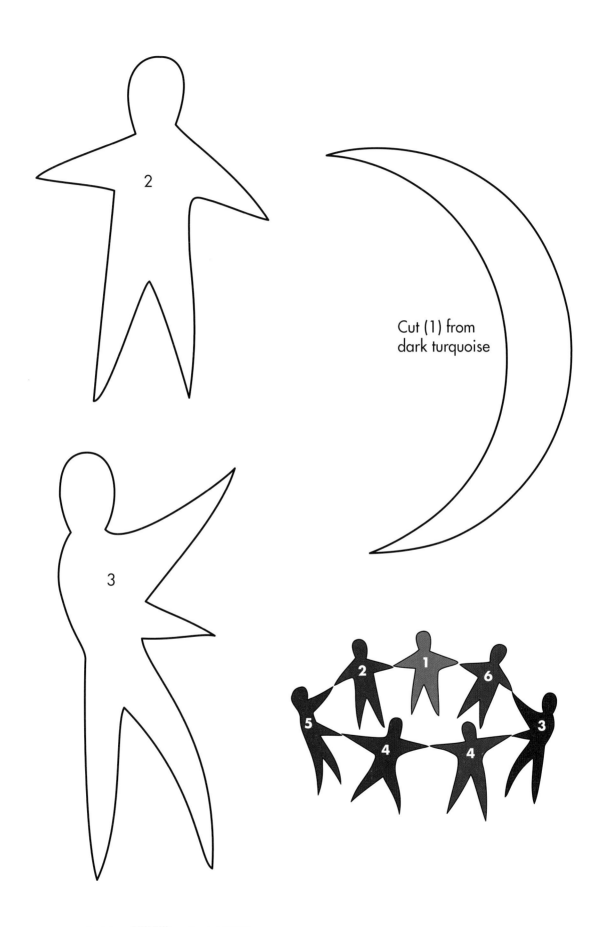

2

Cut (1) from
dark turquoise

3

START YOUR DAY RIGHT! 15½" x 18", made by Janet Saulsbury, Charlottesville, Virginia

START YOUR DAY RIGHT!

Janet Saulsbury took my Quilt University online class and this was what she came up with—in Lesson One! When I was choosing projects for this book, I just knew it had to be included! This wallhanging is the perfect addition to any kitchen nook! So easy to do, you can get it done in an afternoon. Like Janet did, have fun with your embellishments! Start thinking outside the box for ways you can decorate your piece.

Yardage & Cutting Instructions

There truly is no need to go out and purchase fabric for this! (I know we hate to hear that!) There is so little fabric needed, you can surely find what you need in your stash.

For background, cut:
- One 11" x 11" piece from a light print

For the piece below the cup (dark yellow), cut:
- 3½" x 13" strip from a medium fabric

⅜ yard medium print (blue with polka dots), cut:
- Two 3½" x 19" strips (for the side borders)
- Two 3" x 13" strips (for the top and bottom borders)
- Two 2¼" strips (for the binding)

Scraps for the appliqué pieces, cut:
- COFFEE letters that contrast with fabric (They are fused to medium blue print to coordinate with the border.)
- One coffee cup from a medium fabric (pink print)
- One strip for front of cup from a medium fabric (yellow print)
- Other shapes from dark prints (red, dark blue, green)
- Backing: 17" x 20"
- Binding: ¼ yard (match border fabric)

Other Supplies
- Batting: 17" x 20"
- Fusible Web: Fat quarter (396 square inches)
- Assortment of decorative threads (Only one area will be bobbin quilted, so you can stick with the thinner cotton and rayon thread for this project).
- Variety of rickrack
- Small button for center of the daisy
- Invisible thread
- Rotary pinking cutter (optional)
- Wave Edge ruler (optional)

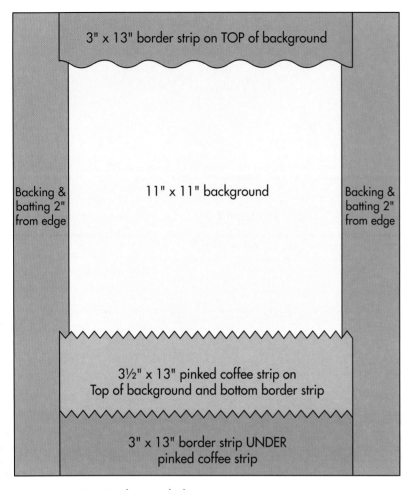

Fig.9–1. Background placement

Within Fig. 9–1:

3" x 13" border strip on TOP of background

11" x 11" background

Backing & batting 2" from edge

Backing & batting 2" from edge

3½" x 13" pinked coffee strip on Top of background and bottom border strip

3" x 13" border strip UNDER pinked coffee strip

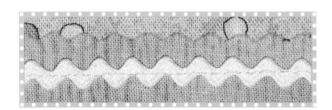

Fig. 9–2

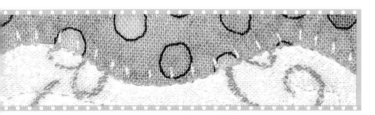

Fig. 9–3

Preparing the Background

1. Iron 2" strips of fusible web to the backs of the long edge of the 3" x 13" top and bottom border strips and the long sides of the 3½" x 19" side border strips.

2. Using a rotary cutter, cut small waves along the fused edge of the top and side border strips using the Wave Edge ruler or freehand.

3. Iron a 3½" strip of fusible web to the back of the 3½" x 13" "coffee" fabric strip. Use a pinking cutter and a ruler to pink both long edges.

4. Layer the backing and batting. Place the 11" x 11" square, the pinked coffee strip, and the top and bottom border strips on top of the batting according to the background placement diagram (Fig. 9–1).

5. Fuse the pieces in place.

The Fun Part!

1. Couch a small contrasting rickrack piece just inside the pinked cut on the 3½" coffee strip. To couch rickrack, stitch a straight line down the middle. Do not use a zigzag stitch (Fig. 9–2).

2. Stitch the top waved border with a buttonhole stitch (Fig. 9–3).

3. Position the side borders, being careful to cover the raw edges. Fuse into place.

4. Couch a contrasting piece of larger rickrack straight down the raw edge of the left border strip, being careful to cover the raw edge (Fig. 9–4).

5. Stitch the right waved border with a buttonhole stitch.

6. Trace, fuse, and cut the remaining pieces (coffee cup, letters, swirls, hearts, flower petals). Following the project picture, position the pieces on the background. When you are satisfied with your placement, fuse in place. Sew a button in the middle of the corner flower.

7. Finish the piece by quilting each fused piece. Use a variety of stitches and threads. Machine quilt inside each letter near its edge (Fig. 9–5).

8. Machine quilt both wavy and straight lines in the borders. Have fun experimenting with different ideas and doodles. Quilt around each heart with invisible thread. Wind the bobbin with thick variegated cotton thread, turn the quilt over and bobbin quilt circles in the hearts for an added pop!

9. Square up and bind with 2¼" strips of the remaining border fabric.

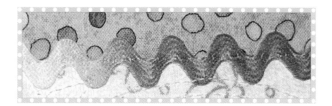

Fig. 9–4

Fig. 9–5

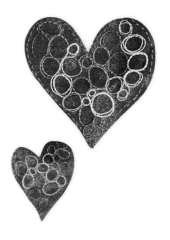

Make 1

Make 1

Make 2

Make 2

Make 1
Top of cup

Make 1
Center of cup

bobbin QUILTIN' & fusin' FUN ✿ MICHELE SCOTT

Make 1 of each to
stimulate steam from cup

Make 1 of each

Make 5 of each for
corner flower

Make 3 of each

Make 1 of each

Make 2 of each

Make 1 of each

HAPPY TOGETHER, 23" x 25½", made by the author

HAPPY TOGETHER

✿ ✿ ✿ ✿ ✿

nspired by my fusing class in which people are encouraged to create something that means something to them, I created this piece to convey the joy I feel when I'm with my family. I have no children, so Lucy the beagle is my child!

Yardage

- Purple batik: ½ yard
  (for background and binding)
- Orange batik: ½ yard for the border
  (strips 4" x 23")
- Solid black: ¼ yard
- Backing: ¾ yard 28" x 25"

Other Supplies

- Batting: 28" x 25"
- Fusible web: 1 yard
  (1,620 square inches)
- Assortment of decorative yarns and
  thread that coordinate with fabrics
- Invisible thread
- Pinking rotary cutter (optional)
- Wave edge ruler (optional)

Cutting Instructions

From the purple, cut:

- One 18" x 22" piece
- Three 2¼" x width-of-fabric strips

From the orange, cut:

- 4 strips 4" x 23"

From the backing fabric, cut:

- one piece 28" x 25"

Piecing the Top

1. Layer the backing, batting, and 18" x 22" background, making sure the background is centered.

2. Iron 2" strips of fusible web on one of the back long edges of the four 4" x 23" border fabric strips.

3. Using a rotary cutter, cut waves on the fused edge of 2 of the strips (for the top and right side borders) using a wave edge ruler or freehand. Use a pinking rotary cutter and a ruler to finish the fused edge of the other 2 strips (for the bottom and left side borders).

4. Position the border strips on top of the layered quilt in this order: top, right side, bottom, left side. When doing it this way, the top border edges are covered by the side borders and the left border overlaps both top and bottom borders. Square up the top, trimming the excess border fabric.

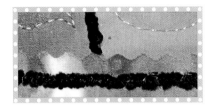

Fig. 10–1

Fig. 10–2

Fig. 10–3

Fig. 10–3

5. Using a contrasting yarn, couch the wavy edge of the top and right border strips. Couch the same yarn just inside the pinked edge of the left and bottom borders (Fig. 10–1).

6. Trace and fuse all templates (pages 83–84) to the back of the black fabric. Cut the pieces out and position them around the piece using the picture as a guide. When satisfied with the placement, fuse to the background.

The Fun Part!

1. To secure all of the black fused pieces, use a free-motion zigzag and a variety of threads for the quilting. For the stars, I used gold metallic (Fig. 10–2).

2. For the flowers, used both solid and variegated rayon thread. For swirls, use a purple metallic (Fig. 10–3).

3. For the family, use a black metallic so they shine (Fig. 10–4). Machine quilt the background with a swirls and points design with matching rayon thread. Quilt the top and right side border with loops in gold metallic. Wind thick cotton variegated thread on your bobbin and quilt a back and forth pattern from the back along the bottom and left side border.

4. Finish by couching a little gold yarn for a collar for the dog (Fig. 10–4).

5. Square up and bind with the 2¼" purple strips.

Cut (1) of each
from black fabric

Cut (3) from black fabric

Cut (1) from black fabric

Cut (3) from black fabric

Cut (3) from black fabric

Cut (4) from black fabric

Cut (3) from black fabric

Cut (2) from black fabric

Cut (3) from black fabric

RISE AND SHINE, 18" x 13", pieced by Barbara Campbell, quilted by the author
(www.loveinstitches.com)

RISE AND SHINE

✿ ✿ ✿ ✿ ✿

What a great way to begin the day with your coffee. These placemats are tremendously easy to make and a great project to try your newly acquired bobbin quilting skills. For matching napkins, visit Barbara Campbell's website, www.loveinstitches.com, and click on Bonus Patterns. Instructions are for four placemats.

Yardage

- Background fabric (ombre gray): 1 yard
- Backing (black): 1 yard
- Sun background (yellow tonal): ½ yard
- Sun rays (assorted orange/gold prints): Four fat quarters

Other Supplies

- Batting: 4 pieces 18" x 13"
- Fusible web: total of 45" x 65" (2,925 square inches)
- Assortment of thick decorative threads/yarns
- Invisible thread

Cutting Instructions

ROTARY CUTTING:

From background fabric, cut:
- Four 18½" x 13½"
From backing fabric, cut:
- Four 18½" x 13½"

TRACE AND FUSE:

- Draw a 14" circle on a piece of paper. Fold in half. This half circle is your sun template. Trace and fuse 4 half circles on yellow fabric.
- 24 Kite Shape A (page 88)

Put it Together

Repeat these steps for each placemat.

1. Position the half circle 3" from the bottom of the background fabric and fuse in place. Position and fuse the kite shapes to the sun (Fig. 11–1).

Fig. 11–1

2. With the placemat right-side up, place the batting and backing right-side down on top—right sides of the placement and batting together. Stitch around all the edges, using a ¼" seam, leaving a 5" opening on the bottom edge for turning. (Note: The batting is cut slightly smaller than the front and back to create less bulk when turning.)

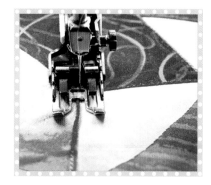

Fig. 11–2

3. Turn the placemat right-side out and stitch the opening closed.

4. Sew around the outside edges with a ¼" seam to secure.

The Fun Part!

1. With invisible thread and a zigzag stitch, couch a thick yarn or cord around the outside of the sun's rays. I used #3 cotton cord from Artfabrik (Fig. 11–2).

Fig. 11–3

2. Echo quilt outside the rays with gold metallic thread and quilt a line along the bottom of the sun. You will need this line of stitching for the bobbin quilting (Fig. 11–3).

3. Wind a bobbin with a thick metallic thread. This project features orange YLI Candlelight. Use a cotton thread in the top that matches the bobbin thread. Machine quilt large swirls and points throughout the sun area (Fig. 11–4).

Fig. 11–4

4. Couch yellow yarn around the sun area and machine quilt waves around the background with a rayon thread that matches the background (Fig. 11–5).

5. *Bon appétit!*

Fig. 11–5

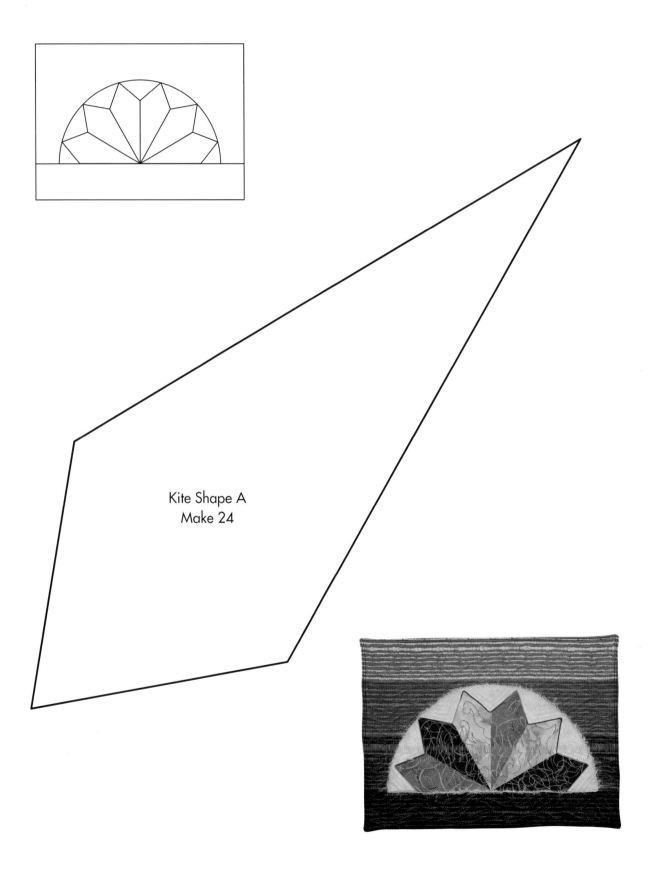

Kite Shape A
Make 24

LAPTOP TOTE, 19½" x 12½" x 2", Designed by Lacey J. Hill, (www.laceyjhill.com)
made by Elinore Locke, Hillsdale, New Jersey

LAPTOP TOTE

❁ ❁ ❁ ❁ ❁

We must look stylish as we tote around out laptop! Have fun with bobbin work as you create this matching set. This is a wonderful first bobbin quilting project because the area being quilted is so small and manageable! In addition, the back is hidden with the lining fabric so you can make all the mess you want on the back and it won't show! Lacey Hill used the gorgeous Garden Party fabric from Yolanda Fundora for Blank. Learn more about Lacey at www.laceyjhill.com.

Yardage

- 1 yard of tote fabric
- 1 yard of lining
- ¾ yard "skirt" fabric for the decorative outside flap
- fat quarter for appliqué flowers
- fat eighth for appliqué flower centers

Keep your scraps—they could make wonderful inside pockets!

Other Supplies

- Batting: 1¾ yard
- Fusible web: total of 8" x 45" (360 square inches)
- Assortment of decorative threads/yarns
- Invisible thread

Cutting Instructions

ROTARY CUTTING:

From tote fabric, cut:
- Two 17" x 22" panels (for the tote)
- Two 4" x width-of-fabric strips (for the straps)

From the lining, cut:
- Two 15" x 20" panels

From the skirt fabric, cut:
- Two 9" x 22" panels (for the skirt)
- Two 7" x 20" panels (for the skirt lining)

From the batting, cut:
- Two 17" x 22" panels (for the tote)
- Two 2" x 40" strips (for the straps)
- Two 8½" x 22" panels (for the skirt)

TRACE AND FUSE:

- 6 Funky Flower A
- 4 Funky Flower B
- 10 Flower Center C

Note: You can use Accuquilt template #55042/ Funky Flowers for the flowers and the Olfa Rotary Circle Cutter for the center circles.

Sewing

1. Place the tote panels right-side up on the batting panels and quilt each panel with a basic allover design. The tote skirt is the focal point, so use a thread that blends with the panels. Trim each panel to measure 20" x 15".

2. Position the 8½" x 22" batting panels on the wrong side of the 9" x 22" skirt panels ½" below the top edge to remove bulk during construction. Pin in place.

NOTE: If any of your flowers overlap the others, fuse and couch the flowers beneath first.

3. Arrange the flowers and flower centers on top of each skirt panel and fuse in place (Fig. 12–1).

4. Couch a decorative yarn with invisible thread on the raw edge of each flower. I used variegated hand-dyed cotton thread (size 3) from Artfabrik (see Resources, page 94).

5. Machine quilt a circular pattern in the flower centers with a matching metallic thread.

6. Prepare the machine with a thick decorative thread in the bobbin (I used YLI Pearl Rayon) and invisible thread on the top. Machine quilt a curlicue meander in the flower petals (Fig. 12–2).

7. Machine quilt the skirt panels with silver metallic thread in a basic meander (from the top or bobbin side). Trim to measure 7" x 20", maintaining the extra ½" of fabric along the top edge.

8. Join the skirt panels along the 7" sides with a ¼" seam allowance, right sides together, keeping the extra ½" of fabric at the top. Join the skirt lining panels along the short ends.

9. Turn the skirt lining unit right-side out and with the skirt unit wrong-side out, insert the lining into the skirt, right sides together, and pin.

10. Stitch the lining and skirt along the edge with the batting with a ¼" seam. Turn right-side out. Pin all the layers of the skirt together and topstitch ¼" from the folded seam.

11. On both tote panels, place a mark 1" in from each bottom corner. Align a rotary ruler with the top corner and the mark along the bottom and trim the edge. Repeat with the lining panels (Fig. 12–3, page 92).

12. Mark a 1" x 1" square at the bottom left and right corners of the tote panels and remove the square with scissors. Repeat with the lining fabrics (Fig. 12–4, page 92).

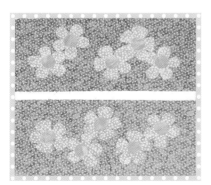

Fig. 12–1

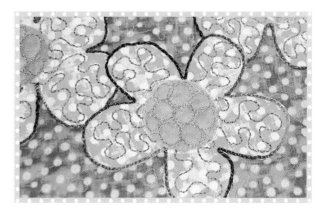

Fig. 12–2

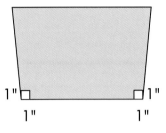

Fig. 12–3

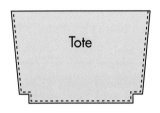

Fig. 12–4

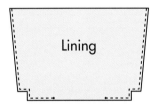

Fig. 12–5

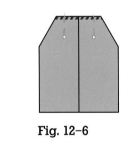

Fig. 12–6

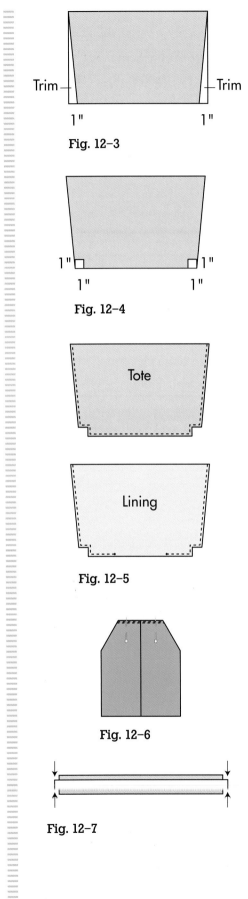

13. With right sides together and ¼" seam allowance, stitch the tote panels together. Back tack at the beginning and end of each seam for stability. Repeat with the lining, leaving a 6" opening at the bottom for turning (Fig. 12–5).

14. To create the tote bottom, align the side seams with the bottom seams to create a straight edge and pin. Stitch ¼" from the edge. Reposition and stitch ⅛" closer to the raw edge for extra stability. Repeat at the other bottom edge (Fig. 12–6).

15. To make the straps, fold the two 4" strips in half lengthwise, wrong sides together. Press well. Open up the strips and place the 2" batting WOF strips centered on the pressed fold. Fold the raw edges into the center to cover the batting (Fig. 12–7).

16. Fold in half again and topstitch through all 6 layers ¼" from both edges. Add a row of stitching down the middle (Fig. 12–8). Trim the straps to the desired length.

Purse Length Minimum 20"
Shoulder Length Minimum 34"

17. Turn the tote right-side out and pin the skirt panels right-side out to the raw edge, matching the side seams and easing in any fullness. Pin the straps 6" in from the outside edges. Baste ¼" from the top edge of the tote (Fig. 12–9, page 93).

18. Insert the tote into the lining with right sides together, and pin well. Stitch all the layers together ½" from the edge. Move the needle ⅛" toward the raw edge and stitch a second row for added strength (Fig. 12–10, page 93).

19. Turn the tote right-side out through the opening in the lining and top stitch ¼" from the edge. Take your time, there are quite a few layers going together. Stitch the opening in the lining closed and you're done (Fig. 12–11, page 93)!

Fig. 12–7

Fig. 12–8

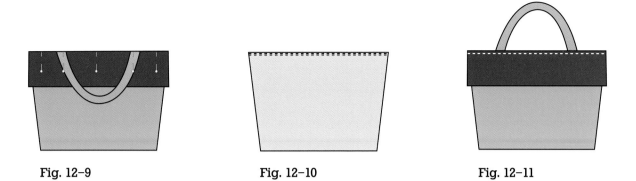

Fig. 12–9   Fig. 12–10   Fig. 12–11

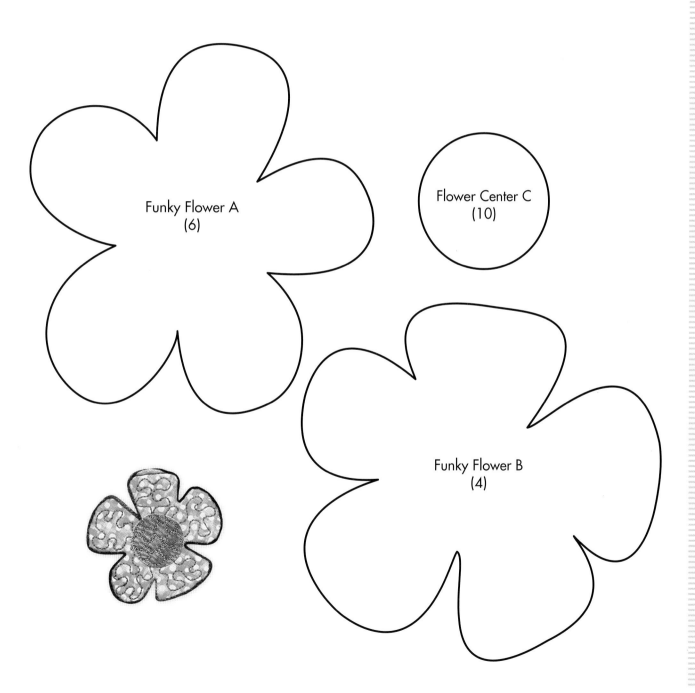

Funky Flower A
(6)

Flower Center C
(10)

Funky Flower B
(4)

Contributors

❀ ❀ ❀ ❀ ❀

Barbara Campbell is a quilt and pattern designer and published author from Pine Brook, New Jersey. She enjoys working with all styles and types of fabric and playing with new techniques. You can see more of her work at www.lovein-stitches.com and her blog— http://DefiningTheInnerMuse.blogspot.com.

Lacey J. Hill, designer, teacher, lecturer, and author is the owner of Golden Thyme Designs, a multi-faceted design studio in New Jersey that encompasses Quilt Design, Wearable Fiber Art, Multi-Media Graphic Design, Color Consultations, and Fashions & Designs for Home Interiors. Learn more about Lacey at www.goldenthymedesigns.com.

Cyndi Souder works mostly with commercial fabric, but that seems to be changing as she likes to stamp and layer her own fabric. She works with texture and embellishments, using beads, old clock parts, and trinkets from the home center. When not in her studio, you can find Cyndi teaching, lecturing, or facilitating workshops. She lives in Northern Virginia with her husband, Eric, and Rowan, her Chesapeake Bay Retriever. Learn more about Cyndi at www.moonlightingquilts.com.

Janet Stophel Saulsbury renewed her interest in quilting in 1990. She is an active member of the Charlottesville Area Quilters Guild, serving as president for four years, and currently dispenses care quilts to community organizations. Janet enjoys both traditional and contemporary quilting and has won awards in local and national contests. She most enjoys donating quilted pieces to raise funds for non-profit organizations. Janet is also a board member of the Virginia Quilt Museum and enjoys volunteering there on a regular basis. She is married, lives in Charlottesville, Virginia, and has three grown children.

Cool Stuff (a.k.a. Resources)

❀ ❀ ❀ ❀ ❀

Here is some information on the people and products that I wrote about. They are just some of my personal favorites!

505 Adhesive Spray
www.sprayandfix.com

Accuquilt Go!
www.accuquilt.com

Artfabrik
www.artfabrik.com

Aurifil
www.aurifil.com

Barbara Campbell
www.lovinstitches.com

Bernina
www.bernina.com

Cyndi Souder
www.moonlightingquilts.com

Clover
www.clover-usa.com

Electric Quilt
www.electricquilt.com

Fairfield
www.poly-fil.com

Golden Threads
www.goldenthreads.com

Horn
www.hornofamerica.com

Lacey Hill
www.laceyjhill.com

Lickity Grip
www.lickitygrip.com

Northcott Silk, Inc.
www.northcott.net

Olfa
www.olfa.com

Quilting Possibilities
Great fabrics and kits!
www.quiltingposs.com

Roxanne Glue Baste It
www.thatperfectstitch.com

Schmetz
www.schmetz.com

Shades of Soft Fuse
www.shadestextiles.com

The Wave Edge™ Ruler
www.thewaveedgeruler.com

Wrights SideWinder
www.wrights.com

YLI
www.ylicorp.com

❖ About the Author ❖

I have been a teacher in the public school system for almost half my life. Approximately thirteen years ago, I decided to take up a little hobby of quilting to pass my time. Like with every other self-respecting "quilt-a-holic," it quickly became a passion. Machine quilting was of particular interest to me, as it was just becoming a popular and acceptable way of quilting your quilt. I was fascinated with the freedom of free-motion quilting, especially creating designs that needed no marking.

Embellishing quilts with a variety of decorative threads was thrilling to me, and I was determined to incorporate as many of them in my quilts as I could! Working with these threads could sometimes be frustrating, so I spent many hours developing strategies to work with them more effectively.

Being a teacher, I was naturally drawn to sharing these methods with my peers. My main goal was to conduct positive, upbeat classes that taught solid techniques and gave all levels of quilters new confidence. For the past 10 years, I have taught at many quilt guilds and shows across the United States and Canada. In addition, I have been on the faculty of the Quilt University, which provides the quilting community with a variety of online classes for quilters.

Photo by Joseph D. Chielli

At the same time that I began lecturing and teaching, I began working with *McCall's Quilting* and *Quick Quilts* magazines. Over the past 10 years, I've had over 50 quilts published in their magazines. Recently, I've begun designing for Fons and Porter and writing for *Quilter's Home* magazine and *Quilter's Choice Network* (QCN), a new online quilting community.

My newest passion is designing fabric for Northcott Silk. I'm currently working on my fifth line of fabric designs with them. Graphic design is a just another way to express my creativity and it's wonderful to use the textiles created in quilts!

A Philadelphia girl at heart, I currently live in South Jersey with my amazingly handsome husband, Tom McColligan, and our dog, Lucy. Life is good.

For more information and free patterns, go to www.piecefulquilter.com.

❀ more AQS Books ❀

This is only a small selection of the books available from the American Quilter's Society. AQS books are known worldwide for timely topics, clear writing, beautiful color photos, and accurate illustrations and patterns. The following books are available from your local bookseller, quilt shop, or public library.

#8532

#8355

#8354

#8353

#8347

#8528

#8242

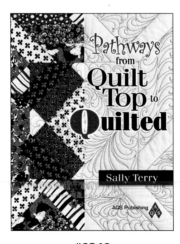

#8348

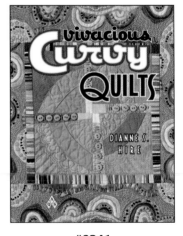

#8241